Interior Maintenance Including Heating, Plumbing and Air Conditioning

New Illustrated Library of Home Improvement Volume 11

Interior Maintenance Including Heating, Plumbing and Air Conditioning

Prentice-Hall/Reston Editorial Staff

Prentice-Hall of Canada, Ltd. / Reston Publishing Company
Scarborough, Ontario

Series contributors/ H. Fred Dale, Richard Demske, George R.
Drake, Byron W. Maguire, L. Donald Meyers, Gershon
Wheeler

Design/ Peter Maher & Associates
Color photographs/ Peter Paterson/Photo Design

Printed and bound in Canada

The publishers wish to thank Alcan Products Limited, Gulf Canada, and Canadian
General Electric for providing photographs for this volume.

Contents

Chapter 1   **Materials and Joints 11**
- 1-1.   Lumber   11
- 1-2.   Plywood   14
- 1-3.   Wood Joints   14
- 1-4.   Adhesives   16
- 1-5.   Panelling   17
- 1-6.   Aluminum   17
- 1-7.   Wall Fasteners   17

Chapter 2   **Doors 20**
- 2-1.   The Parts of a Door   20
- 2-2.   How to Fix a Broken Door   21
- 2-3.   How to Hang a Door   23
- 2-4.   Locks and Latches   25
- 2-5.   How to Cure Door Troubles   26

Chapter 3   **Glass 28**
- 3-1.   How to Replace Glass   28
- 3-2.   Sash Cords   30
- 3-3.   Stuck Windows   31

Chapter 4   **Stairs 34**
- 4-1.   Construction of Stairs   34

4-2. Squeaky Stairs 34
4-3. Replacing Treads 35

Chapter 5   Floors 37
5-1. Wood Floors 37
5-2. How to Install a New Threshold 39
5-3. How to Refinish Wood Floors 40
5-4. How to Lay a Wood Floor over Concrete 42
5-5. How to Lay Flexible Tiles 43
5-6. How to Lay Linoleum 47
5-7. How to Lay Ceramic Tiles 49

Chapter 6   Walls and Ceilings 50
6-1. Wall Finishes 50
6-2. How to Patch Plaster 51
6-3. How to Build a Wall 51
6-4. How to Fur a Wall 54
6-5. How to Tile a Wall 54
6-6. How to Repair a Tiled Wall 55
6-7. How to Install Shelves 55
6-8. Wallpaper 56
6-9. How to Remove Old Wallpaper 57
6-10. How to Hang Wallpaper 57

Chapter 7   Plumbing 59
7-1. How to Shut Off the Water Supply 59
7-2. Frozen Pipes 60
7-3. Leaks in Water Pipes 60
7-4. Dripping Faucets 63
7-5. How to Add a Faucet 64
7-6. Types of Pipe 65
7-7. Noisy Plumbing 67
7-8. Traps and Vents 69
7-9. Clogged Plumbing 71
7-10. Toilet Tanks 75
7-11. Toilet Tank Repairs 77

Chapter 8   Climate Control 80
8-1.   Furnaces   82
8-2.   Hot-Air Systems   86
8-3.   Hot-Water Systems   90
8-4.   Steam Heat   94
8-5.   Radiant Heat   98
8-6.   Insulation   99
8-7.   Storm Windows and Doors   102
8-8.   Weather Stripping   104
8-9.   Attic Fans   106

Chapter 9   Electricity 107
9-1.   Fundamentals   107
9-2.   Safety   114
9-3.   How to Replace a Wall Switch   115
9-4.   How to Replace a Receptacle   117
9-5.   Cords and Connectors   117
9-6.   Doorbells   123

Materials and Joints

The most common building material in your house is probably wood, and wood is used for many of the repair jobs that you will do. In addition, you will also use wallboard, tiles, adhesives and an assortment of other materials. In many cases you will have a choice of material. To choose wisely, you should know the pros and cons.

1-1. Lumber

You can save money on lumber if you buy the right wood for the job. Typically, you can use inferior finishes where wood doesn't show, as inside walls or under floors. Even where finish is important, you may be able to economize by buying boards with knotholes and cutting the wood you need from the length between imperfections. You must decide what wood you want as well as what grade.

Wood from broadleaf trees is generally harder than wood from trees with needles. Pine, fir, redwood, cedar, and the like are called *softwoods;* ash, oak, mahogany, walnut, and other broadleaf trees are *hardwoods.* Hardwoods are usually stronger than softwoods but are also more difficult to work with. There are some exceptions, however. Gumwood and poplar, both classed as hardwoods, are easy to work and not very strong.

Table 1-1 lists some common woods and their characteristics. For structural jobs, you will want woods resistant to moisture and decay. Workability is always a consideration. If you will be driving many nails or screws into a board, you will want the wood to be easy to work with. For general construction, softwoods are generally used, whereas hardwoods are chosen for furniture and decorative trim. Moldings are usually made of pine, and dowels of birch.

Lumber is graded according to quality by numbers or letters. The highest quality is #1 for numbers, or grade A for letters. Grade designations are indicated in Table 1-2. You should not use grade #5, and use #4 only for temporary structures, such as concrete forms or props.

Another consideration in selection of lumber is the direction of the grain in structural pieces. The grain is specified as *flat* if it is parallel to the wide dimensions of the cross section of a board and *vertical* if it is perpendicular to the wide dimensions. Flat-grained lumber, as shown in Figure 1-1(a), is stronger than the vertically grained lumber shown in Figure 1-1(b), but may be selected on the basis of appearance.

Lumber sizes are usually specified as the size before drying and milling the boards. Thus, a board said to be 1″ thick may in fact be only 3/4″ thick. If you want specific sizes, specify *actual* rather than *nominal* dimen-

Table 1-1. Characteristics of Woods

Wood	Hard or Soft	Moisture Resistance	Decay Resistance	Workability	Strength
Ash	H	Fair	Excellent	Difficult	Excellent
Birch	H	Fair	Fair	Difficult	Excellent
Cedar	S	Good	Excellent	Good	Fair
Cypress	S	Good	Excellent	Good	Fair
Douglas fir	S	Poor	Poor	Easy	Good
Mahogany	H	Excellent	Excellent	Difficult	Excellent
Maple	H	Excellent	Good	Difficult	Good
Oak	H	Excellent	Good	Difficult	Excellent
Pine	S	Good	Poor	Easy	Good
Poplar	H	Fair	Poor	Easy	Fair
Redwood	S	Good	Excellent	Easy	Fair
Spruce	S	Good	Poor	Easy	Fair
Walnut	H	Excellent	Good	Difficult	Good

Table 1-2. Grades of Lumber

Grade	Description
{ # 1 and # 2 Clear, A and B }	Almost entirely free of imperfections; best quality
C Select	Small imperfections which can take a fine paint job
D Select	Lowest grade suitable for painting
# 1 Common	Some small knots; can be used without waste
# 2 Common	Slightly larger knots than # 1 Common; no waste
# 3	Larger knots; pitch; some waste
# 4	Big knots; pitch; not durable
# 5	Knotholes; loose knots

sions. Lumber is usually sold by the board foot calculated as the product of the thickness in inches times the width in feet times the length in feet. These are nominal dimensions. For example, a board nominally 3/4″ thick, 10″ wide, and 4′ long would be 3/4 × 10/12 × 4 = 2-1/2 board feet. Occasionally, lumberyards have sales of specific sizes or grades, and if you can use them, you may save money buying the sale material instead of the exact wood you need.

In addition to flat boards and structural

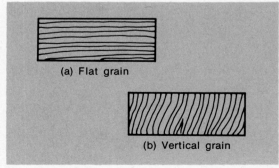

(a) Flat grain

(b) Vertical grain

Fig. 1-1. Grain.

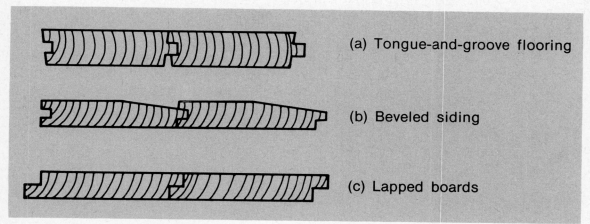

(a) Tongue-and-groove flooring

(b) Beveled siding

(c) Lapped boards

Fig. 1-2. Boards for special applications.

pieces such as 2″ × 4″s or 4″ × 10″s, lumberyards carry stock for special purposes. Three examples are shown in Figure 1-2. Tongue-and-groove flooring, shown in Figure 1-2(a), is for finished floors. Note the slight bevel at the joint so that a good contact can be ensured at the surface of the floor. Beveled siding, in Figure 1-2(b), is used for sides of houses. Other similar sidings are also available. The lapped boards in Figure 1-2(c) have a number of applications where a tight joint is required. Special shapes available for decorative purposes are shown in Figure 1-3. A few of the almost unlimited variety of shapes for moldings are shown in Figure 1-3(a). Decorative strips for valances and other uses are shown in Figure 1-3(b). Again, there is a large and growing variety of these. Table legs and balusters, in Figure 1-3(c), are a few of the turned shapes. The uses for the many varieties of shapes supplied by your lumber dealer are limited only by your imagination. For example, you might want to use pieces of molding or lengths of a closet rod as shelf props in a bookcase.

If you use poorer-grade lumber, don't throw away sections of boards with loose knots. Frequently you can tighten the knots with glue and save some material. Invariably you will have some extra lengths of wood or scraps when you have a carpentry project, and you will wonder whether to save them. Scraps of decorative trim and moldings should be kept. Scraps of ordinary boards should be saved up

to a point: these pieces make good sanding blocks, but how many do you need? Use a cardboard carton for these scraps, and when it gets too full, use some of the scraps for burning in your fireplace. Larger pieces should always be saved, since you can cut needed small pieces from a good larger one. Pieces of structural lumber, 2″ × 4″s and larger, and pieces of plywood should be saved, because these are stronger materials that can be used for braces.

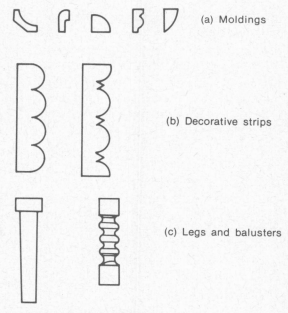

(a) Moldings

(b) Decorative strips

(c) Legs and balusters

Fig. 1-3. Special shapes.

1-2. Plywood

Plywood consists of several layers, or *plies*, of wood bonded together with glue and having the grains in adjacent plies perpendicular to each other. A given thickness of plywood is much stronger than the same thickness of a solid board of the same wood. Douglas fir is the most common material for plywood, but plywood with hardwood faces is available for cabinet work and other decorative applications. Fir plywood comes in *exterior* type, which is waterproof, and *interior* type, which would deteriorate if subjected to the elements for too long.

The wood in plywood is graded by letters, as follows:

a. Fine appearance.

b. Smooth, can be painted.

c. Contains knotholes or splits.

d. Large knotholes.

The inner plies are usually grade C in exterior plywood and may be grade D in the interior type. The designated grade indicates the surface plies, which can be A, B, or C in exterior and even D in interior. The surface plies do not have to be the same. Thus, A-B interior plywood has grade A on the front, grade B on the back and grade D for all inner plies. Don't buy A-A if one side will not be seen. For structural uses, you can buy the lowest available grade, C-D.

When sawing plywood, it is almost impossible to prevent a ragged edge on one side, caused when the sawtooth emerges from the wood. Therefore, always saw on the better side. If both sides will be exposed, use a fine saw to minimize the roughness.

The edge of a plywood board may be covered with decorative moldings sold specifically for the purpose or with a special filler, applied like putty. The best solution is plywood *edging tape*, a thin, flexible tape made of wood. It is available in fir, mahogany, walnut, etc., and has an adhesive backing. Stick the tape to the edge of the plywood, and apply heat with a warm iron against the tape. Instructions come with the tape. If the tape protrudes beyond the surface of the plywood, sand it off, using fine sandpaper around a small block of wood.

1-3. Wood Joints

The most common wood joint is a *butt* joint, where two pieces of wood are simply butted against one another (Figure 1-4). The joint can be held by nails or screws. Screws are stronger than nails in a butt joint, but for additional strength, one of the joints shown in Figure 1-5 should be used. The *rabbeted joint*, in Figure 1-5(a), is stronger than a butt joint, since the horizontal board is supported by the rabbet. The *dado*, or slot, in the vertical member in Figure 1-5(b) gives additional

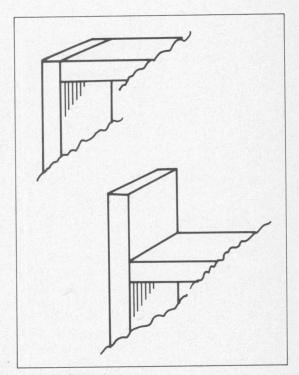

Fig. 1-4. Butt joints.

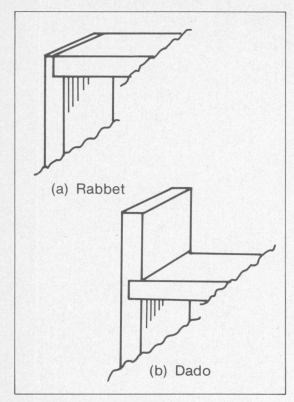

Fig. 1-5. Rabbet and dado joints.

support and is excellent for shelves. Both the rabbet and dadoed joints should be secured with nails or screws *and* a strong glue. The miter joint, in Figure 1-6(a), is used for appearances and is not very strong, although it can be strengthened by the addition of a block in contact with both boards, as shown. Nails and glue must be used in a mitered joint. Dowels, shown in Figure 1-6(b), are stronger than screws when properly applied. They can be used with butts, rabbets or dadoes.

A rabbet can be cut with a handsaw, power saw or sabre saw. A dado is best made with a power saw but can be made with a chisel. For doweling, use a drill the same size as the dowels, about half the thickness of the boards being joined. Drill through both pieces simultaneously, holding them together and making sure that the hole is at least 1 inch into the inner piece. Cut the dowel to length so that when its end is flush with the outside surface, it will protrude 1 inch into the inner piece. Coat the contacting surfaces of the boards,

and also the dowel, with glue. Drive the dowel into the hole, using a scrap block of wood on the end so that your hammer will not mar the surface of the board. It will be easier to drive in the dowel if you round the top slightly with a file or sandpaper.

The *mortise and tenon* is a strong joint used in window screens and furniture. The parts of the joint are shown in Figure 1-7. The *tenon*, in Figure 1-7(a), is a tongue extension cut on the end of one piece to be joined. The *mortise*, shown in Figure 1-7(b), is a rectangular opening cut in the second piece to receive the tenon. The two parts must fit closely and are glued. If a joint is to be concealed, a *blind mortise* is used, as shown in Figure 1-7(c). The rectangular mortise goes only partly through the second piece, and the tenon is cut shorter.

The tenon can be cut easily with an all-purpose saw or any small handsaw. First, mark the outline of the tenon on all the surfaces of the piece to be cut, as in Figure 1-8(a). Then, cut on all lines with the saw,

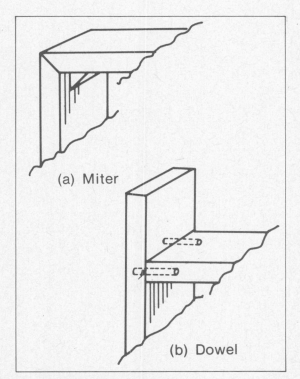

Fig. 1-6. Miter and dowel joints.

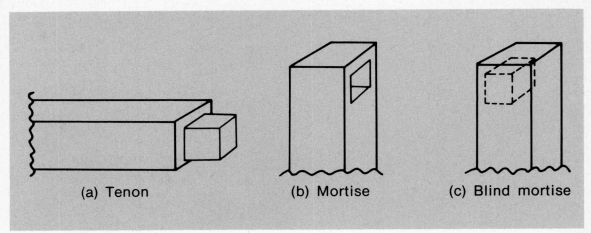

Fig. 1-7. Mortise and tenon.

leaving the tenon on the end. To make a mortise, first mark the outline, as in Figure 1-8(b), then drill out as much material as possible. Finish both parts with a chisel and sandpaper, making frequent trials to ensure a good fit.

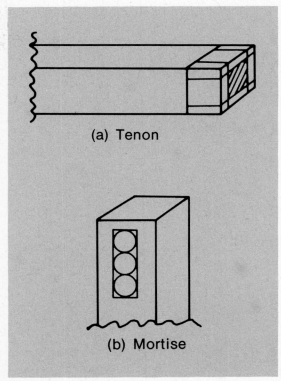

Fig. 1-8. Cutting mortise and tenon.

1-4. Adhesives

Animal glues are rarely used today because better adhesives have been developed. However, with the wide variety of adhesives available, it is sometimes hard to tell which is the best for a particular job.

The most popular glue is white poly (vinyl acetate). This is a milky liquid, usually packaged in squeeze bottles, and it dries clear. This adhesive can be used for bonding wood and most porous materials, such as paper, cloth, leather or cork. It should not be used for metal or plastics. The glue sets in half an hour and reaches full strength in 24 hours. It is *not* waterproof. When applying this adhesive, the temperature of the materials and the room in which you work should be at least 70° F.

For stronger joints or in applications requiring a waterproof bond, plastic resin glue should be used. It too must be worked in temperatures above 70° F. These glues set in about six hours, so the bond must be well clamped.

The strongest adhesives are epoxy cements. They are expensive and harder to apply. You must mix two materials together and apply immediately. Parts must be clamped for about ten hours. A working temperature above 70° F is again required.

If you must do your gluing in a cold cellar or garage, you will have to use casein glue. It comes in powdered form and is mixed with water as needed. It forms a strong bond on wood but is not waterproof.

When you are gluing, make sure that the contact surfaces are clean and dry. Scrape or sand off any layer of old glue or paint which would prevent the new glue from reaching the porous surface. Follow the instructions on the label for mixing and applying the new glue. Especially important are temperature restrictions. After gluing, clamp the joint so that parts stay in contact. If clamps cannot be used because of odd shapes, use your ingenuity to devise ways of holding the bond together with rope or strips of cloth.

For special jobs, such as laying tiles or linoleum, use the adhesive recommended by the supplier. It will be designed for the materials involved, though it may not be very effective on wood.

1-5. Panelling

In addition to solid wood and plywood, you can get large panels made of hardboard, gypsum wallboard, or plastic laminate, for use in your home. They are all easy to apply and extremely durable.

Hardboard is made of pulverized wood fibers processed into a dense, rigid material. The outside surfaces can be covered in a wide variety of finishes, including simulated wood, leather, plastic, or any color of paint or enamel. Hardwood panels are available in sheets up to 4 by 8 feet, in thicknesses of 1/4″ or 1/8″. They can be used for wall panels, counter tops, bench tops, and even floors and doors. When nailed, edges must be supported. Nails should be at least 1″ long, spaced 4″ apart. Hardboard can be cut with a saw, drilled, planed and sanded.

Gypsum wallboard, for walls and ceilings, consists of plaster between two layers of cardboard. It is available in sizes up to 4′ by 12′ and thicknesses up to 1/2″. The board can be cut easily by scoring with a knife and breaking it along the mark. It can be nailed, but care must be taken not to break the paper.

In normal application, wallboards are nailed to studs, and the seams between adjacent boards are filled with joint cement. The joint is covered with tape, a second thin layer of cement is applied, and finally it is sanded to be ready for painting. Although wallboard is cheap, more care is required than with hardwood.

Plastic laminate is more expensive than other panelling but it makes an attractive surface which is easy to clean. Further, it needs no finishing. It comes in 1/16″ sheets for most applications, but for small jobs 1/32″ material is also available. It can be scored with a knife and broken to size. A special adhesive supplied with the laminate cements it in place.

1-6. Aluminum

Aluminum is not thought of as a building material, but it is now available in so many sizes and shapes that it can be used in many odd jobs around the home. It is found in sheets, rods, bars, tubing, and angles, as well as in many decorative designs. Some alloys are soft enough to be worked with ordinary woodworking tools. You can use aluminum angles for structural pieces, such as in frames for tables or supports for shelves. Round or rectangular tubing can be used for table legs and awning supports. Aluminum channels can be used as window guides. Special parts for the home include aluminum gutters and aluminum siding. Aluminum sheets can be cut with scissors or metal shears. Soft aluminum bars and tubing can be cut with a handsaw, harder alloys with a hacksaw or all-purpose saw. Aluminum can be drilled, nailed, planed and painted.

1-7. Wall Fasteners

There are many different types of fastenings for attaching to a wall anything from a light picture to a heavy cabinet, and new types keep appearing. For a specific job, ask the advice of your building materials supplier. Some of the more common fasteners are described below.

You can use ordinary nails or screws if you can fasten the material to be hung to a wall stud or part of the framework of a house. For a large cabinet this is the first choice. Remember that studs are 16 inches apart between centers. You can sometimes locate studs by tapping on the wall. There is a hollow sound between studs and a solid feel right at the stud. If you have difficulty, buy an inexpensive stud locator, available in most hardware stores, and follow the instructions.

If you have to locate something heavy between studs, you may be able to use a "bridge" for reinforcement, as shown in Figure 1-9. Locate the studs and screw a flat board to the studs. The board should be about 18″ long and at least 1″ × 4″. Heavy objects can then be supported from any part of the board. For something very heavy, use a longer board attached to three or more studs.

For lightweight objects, such as toothbrush holders, towel racks, small pictures, and the like, there are many hangers available. Some are simply pushed into plaster walls with the

fingers or held in place with a thin brad. Some are glued in place. Towel racks and other bathroom fittings usually come with their own fasteners and instructions for installing.

For heavier pictures and mirrors up to about 40 pounds, you can use a simple picture hook. This is fastened by a nail held in the hook at an angle to the wall. On plaster walls, stick transparent tape where the nail is to enter, to keep the plaster from cracking. These hooks come in a variety of sizes, graded according to the weight they will support.

When it is necessary to fasten a heavy weight to a hollow wall, screws or nails do not furnish enough support, since the portion in the wall is a small part of the total length of the screw. There are three types of fasteners especially for hollow walls (Figure 1-10). The *toggle bolt*, in Figure 1-10(a) and (b), has wings normally held open by springs. A hole must be drilled in the wall large enough to insert the bolt with wings folded. The fixture to be hung must be placed on the bolt first and then the wings. The wings are pushed through the hole in the wall, as in Figure 1-10(a), and the wings are opened by the springs when they are inside the wall. The wings are pressed firmly against the inside of the wall when the bolt is tightened, as in Figure 1-10(b). One disadvantage of this type of fastener is that if the bolt is removed to take off the fixture, the wings fall inside the wall and cannot be retrieved.

The *expansion screw anchor*, usually called a *molly* anchor, is shown in Figure 1-10(c) and (d). It consists of a thin metal sleeve and a machine screw. The hole required in the wall can be smaller than that for a toggle bolt. The molly anchor is inserted as shown in Figure 1-10(c), and when the screw is tightened, the sleeve deforms, as shown in Figure 1-10(d). Now the screw can be removed, and the sleeve remains in place. The screw can be reinserted with a fixture mounted on it.

The *plug*, shown in Figure 1-10(e), may be made of plastic, lead, or fibrous material and is simply a hollow sleeve, inserted in a closefitting hole in the wall, which accepts an ordinary wood screw. The hole through the

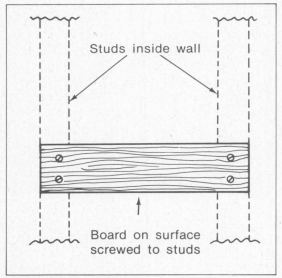

Fig. 1-9. Bridging studs.

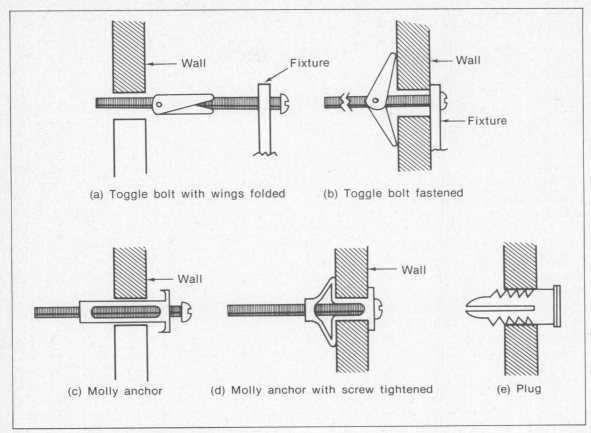

Fig. 1-10. Fasteners for hollow walls.

center is tapered with the narrow end inside the wall. When a screw is driven into the plug, the plug expands, tightening its hold on the wall. The inner end also expands against the inside of the wall to increase the holding power.

Permanent fasteners for masonry walls and floors use the expansion principle of the plug shown in Figure 1-10(e). These anchors for masonry are made of plastic or lead for smaller bolts and of steel to accept heavy lag screws. Unlike the plug, they are entirely contained in the hole in the masonry and, when expanded, grip firmly. To install an expansion anchor, first a hole must be drilled in the masonry. You can use a *star drill*, which is essentially a cold chisel with two cutting edges at right angles to each other. It is held in place with one hand and struck with a heavy hammer. A simpler method is to use a special masonry bit in an electric drill. These are available in sizes up to 1/2 inch, but with 1/4-inch shanks so that they can be used in 1/4-inch electric drills. When drilling, press firmly so that the masonry bit does not slip. Slipping tends to dull the bit.

2 Doors

2-1. The Parts of a Door

To understand instructions or fixing door troubles, you must be familiar with the terms used by carpenters to describe the various parts of a door and door frame (Figure 2-1). These terms are used frequently in how-to-do-it books, but unless they are defined, the home repairman may find the instructions difficult to follow.

Horizontal bars are called *rails*. In the figure there are three rails. Vertical bars are *stiles*. The thin portions of the door between stiles and rails are called *panels*. If a door is solid, it has no rails and stiles, and the door may be thought of as one large panel. A hollow door has a framework of stiles and rails which is completely covered with thin veneer sheets on both sides to give the appearance of a solid door.

The doorknob and latch are on one edge of the door, and the hinges are on the opposite edge. The door frame is usually mortised or cut out to accommodate the hinge so that the surface of the hinge is flush with the surface of the edge of the door. The mortised recess for the hinge is called a *gain*, as indicated in Figure 2-1. A typical hinge is shown in Figure 2-2. One leaf is attached to a gain in the door and the other to a gain in the door frame. A removable pin joins the two leaves of the hinge. There is usually an ornamental knob attached to the hinge similar to the knob at the top of the pin, but since the ornamental knob has no functional purpose, it is sometimes omitted. A hole through the knob permits access to the bottom of the pin. Most doors have two hinges, but heavy outside doors in your home may require three.

Part of a door frame is shown in Figure 2-3. The parts of the frame next to the sides and

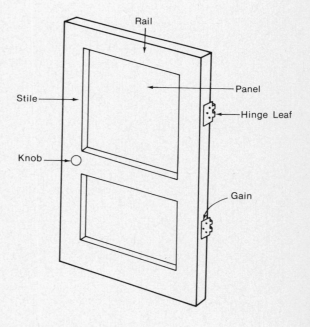

Fig. 2-1. Parts of a door.

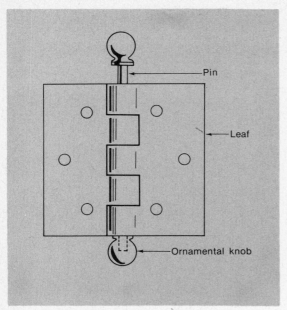

Fig. 2-2. Door hinge.

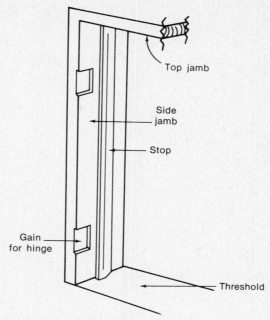

Fig. 2-3. Door frame.

top of the door are called *jambs*. Fastened to the jambs are *stops*, which are simply strips of wood to limit the movement of the door. The door is in contact with the stops when it is closed. The jamb on the latch side of the door

The threshold of an outside door should be varnished to protect it from rain and snow.

has a gain cut into it to accommodate the *striker plate*, which engages the latch. This plate is mounted with its surface flush with the surface of the jamb.

The bottom of the doorway is called the *threshold*. For outside doors the threshold is usually a board under the door, but inside the house, floors may be continuous from one room to another without a raised threshold.

2-2. How to Fix a Broken Door

Doors take a lot of abuse, but with a little imagination, damage can be covered up, and broken doors can be repaired inexpensively. The repaired door may not be as good as new, but it will function as it is supposed to, and only a critical eye could detect the repair work.

When the veneer of a hollow door is broken, for example, from bumping into a piece of furniture or from being bumped by a tricycle, you can glue a new layer on top of the old veneer and hide the hole completely. If the

Drilling holes for dowels in cracked door.

damage is on the side of the door which contacts the stops, the extra thickness would not permit the door to close. Simply cut the new veneer to leave a margin of about 2″ to 6″ all around it. The new veneer will then look like a decorative panel on the door. You might like it so much that you will want to glue a similar "panel" to the other side of the door. If only a small part of the door is damaged, use a patch of decorative veneer to cover it. Veneers are available in many colors and with a variety of designs. Follow the manufacturer's instructions to install the veneer, since some come with an adhesive backing.

A more serious problem is a broken stile on the hinge side of the door. This can happen to any door that is banged too hard, but storm doors are especially susceptible. If the door is only cracked, you can glue the parts together again. Pry open the crack, as in Figure 2-4. Place a chisel or screwdriver near the bottom of the crack to hold the two surfaces apart.

Coat the surfaces with adhesive. If the door is a storm door or other outside door, use waterproof glue or any of the new adhesives that can withstand the weather. Remove the chisel, and squeeze the two parts of the crack together. Tie strips of an old sheet around the door to hold the crack closed until the glue dries.

When a more durable repair job is required, such as when a piece of the door is broken off completely, you can use dowels (wooden rods) to hold the two pieces together solidly (Figure 2-5). First, glue the two parts together by coating the surfaces of the breaks with glue. Now drill holes for dowels along the edge of the door. These holes should be about 5″ or 6″ apart and should be deep enough to penetrate the larger section about 2″. The diameter of the dowels depends on the thickness of the door. For thick doors use 1/2″ dowels and drill 1/2″ holes for them. For doors less than 1″ thick, thinner dowels can

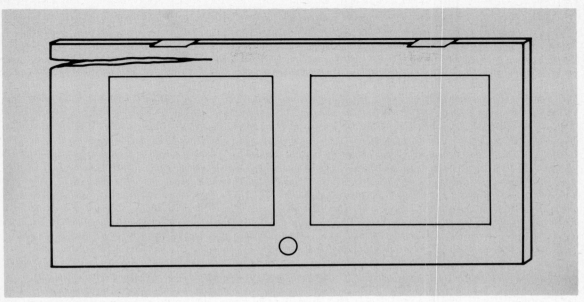

Fig. 2-4. Crack in door.

be used. Cut the dowels to length so that they will extend at least 1-1/2″ beyond the crack. Coat the dowels with glue, and then tap them in with a hammer so that the ends are flush with the edge of the door. When the glue on the dowels dries, the repaired door will be as sturdy as new. The only difficult part of this job is drilling the holes for the dowels straight without coming out the side of the door. If you stand astride the door as you drill, it is fairly simple to hold the drill parallel to the faces of the door.

If the split is under a hinge, you may want to move the hinge. Cut a new gain, as described in the next section, a few inches above or below the old mortise, and install the hinge there. The old gain can be covered with a

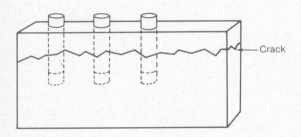

Fig. 2-5. Repairing door with dowels.

scrap of wood which is cut to fit. Fasten the block with glue or brads, or both. Drive the head of each brad below the surface with a nailset and fill the hole with putty or wood filler. Also use filler in the cracks around the block if it is not an exact fit. When the block and jamb are repainted, they will look like one solid piece.

2-3. How to Hang a Door

The cost of labor for installing a new door is frequently more than the cost of the door itself. It therefore pays to hang a door yourself. With a little care you can do a professional job.

First, the door must be fitted to the opening. If you are lucky, you may be able to buy a door which is just the right size, but more likely you will have to settle for one that is larger than the doorway and trim it down. You should allow about 1/16″ at the top and two sides. For an outside door, allow about 1/4″ to 1/2″ clearance above the threshold. The space is not critical, since you will cover it with a drip cap and weather stripping. For an inside door

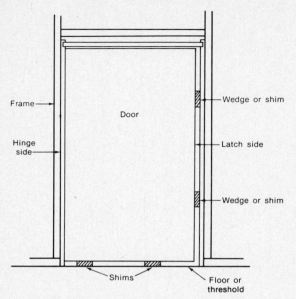

Fig. 2-6. Positioning door for locating hinges.

without a raised threshold, allow at least 3/8″ at the bottom, and more if the door has to clear linoleum, a rug or an irregular floor. A space of up to 1″ at the bottom of an inside door is no problem.

If you have to trim off only a small amount to make a door fit, use a plane. Plane the bottom first, and then along one side. When planing across the grain, usually at the bottom of the door, do not run the blade of the plane off the side, since it may splinter the edge. Plane from both edges toward the middle. This is not a problem when planing with the grain. If you have to take off more than about 1/4″ of wood, you can saw off the excess and then touch up the surface with a plane or sandpaper to smooth it.

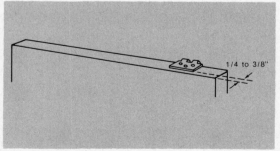

Fig. 2-7. Marking hinge position.

If you are replacing a door, you can use the same hinges that were used on the old door and in the same locations on the jamb. You will have to cut new mortises or gains for the hinges only on the door itself. If you are hanging a new door, you will have to cut mortises in both the jamb and the door, and you will have to buy hinges. When buying hinges, tell your hardware dealer the size and thickness of the door, and let him show you a selection of appropriate hinges. The next problem is locating the hinges. Place the door in the opening and prop it up with pieces of wood, cardboard, or anything handy, so that it is correctly positioned in the opening. Now wedge some thin pieces of wood on the latch side so that the door is shoved tightly against the hinge jamb, as shown in Figure 2-6. If there are hinges already on the jamb, mark their positions accurately with a sharp pencil on the door. If this is a new installation, jab the point of a sharp knife held horizontally in the crack between the door and the jamb so that it marks both simultaneously. The top hinge can be anywhere from 6″ to 9″ from the top of the door, and the bottom hinge can be 6″ to 1′ from the floor. After you have marked the location of the hinges, take down the door.

Place a leaf of a hinge on the edge of the door, as in Figure 2-7, and using it as a pattern, mark around it with a sharp knife. The inside edge of the hinge should be 1/4″ to 3/8″ from the edge of the door, as in Figures 2-6 and 2-7. The exact dimension is not critical, but it should be noted carefully, and the corresponding dimension on the jamb (from the hinge to the stop) should be the same or a hair larger. The positions of the mortises are then located on the door, as in Figure 2-8. Similar outlines are drawn on the jamb. Support the door solidly with its hinge edge up. Do not try to cut out the mortise in one piece. Drive a chisel along the edges of the large face of the mortised piece with the bevel pointing inward. Make several additional cuts with your chisel across the face of the mortise, as shown by the dotted lines in Figure 2-8. Finally, drive your chisel into the side *with the bevel up,* cutting out the mortise in small chunks. If you happen to cut the mortise too deep, place a piece of cardboard

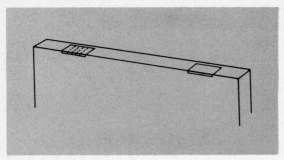

Fig. 2-8. Cutting mortises.

under the hinge when you mount it. Cut the gains in the jamb in the same manner. Screw the hinge leaves in their proper positions. Now lift the door so that the leaves intermesh and drop in the hinge pins. Installing a latch and striker plate is discussed in Section 2-4.

As soon as you can, after hanging a new door, make sure that you coat all surfaces with a primer to prevent moisture absorption which could warp the door or cause it to swell. A final paint or varnish coating can be done more leisurely, as long as the surface is protected.

2-4. Locks and Latches

After a new door is hung, a latch or lock must be added. Many old-fashioned locks require large mortises to be cut out of the edge of the door, but modern locks can be installed in round holes. To install a modern lock you need only a brace and assorted bits. When you buy a lock, you will also receive a template, which will enable you to locate the position of the holes to be drilled accurately. Drill sizes are also indicated in the instructions with the lock set. When you drill through the door, drill from one side only until the point of the bit just emerges from the opposite side. Then pull out the drill and finish the job by drilling into the door from the opposite side. If you were to drill all the way through from one side, the emerging drill could split the wood.

If you want to use a lock that requires a large mortise, drill out as much material as possible (Figure 2-9), and then finish the job with a chisel. The body of the lock goes into the opening, and an additional gain must be cut around the opening to accommodate the plate of the lock. The surface of the lock should be flush with the edge of the door.

The striker plate is mounted on the jamb. In addition to the gain cut for the striker, you must cut out extra material for the bolt or latch to enter. Again, the job is simplified if you follow the instructions and use the templates furnished with the lock set. If you happen to cut too deep a mortise for the striker plate, use cardboard to shim it up flush with the surface of the jamb.

Some doors are never locked, and some need no inside handle to close them. For example, a door in a hall closet does not need a lock and can do without an inside knob. In such cases, you can use a spring latch, which requires neither mortising nor drilling. A hook is attached near the top of the door, and the spring latch is fastened to the upper jamb to mate with the hook when the door is closed. A knob is fastened to the outside of the door to pull it open. The latch holds the door closed, but a slight pull disengages the latch. Such a latch is very easy to install.

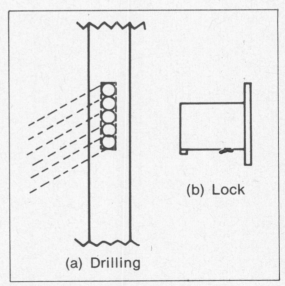

(b) Lock

(a) Drilling

Fig. 2-9. Drilling a mortise for a lock.

2-5. How to Cure Door Troubles

When a door sticks, the trouble may be caused by settling of the house and a resultant distortion of the frame around the door, by swelling of the wood due to moisture, or by one or more loose hinges. Don't be in a hurry to use a plane to try to make the door fit. Planing a door that has swelled from too much moisture may make the door easy to open again, but when the moisture dries out, the door may then shrink and be too small for the opening. This is especially noticeable in areas that have well-defined rainy seasons. In such climates, it is important that all surfaces of the door, including edges, be protected from moisture by painting them regularly. Coating the edges with paraffin also helps.

The first thing to do when a door sticks is to check the hinges. A loose hinge will allow the door to tilt in the frame. Tighten all screws. If screws turn too freely because the thread in the wood is stripped, you should fill the screw hole with wood filler. If you have no wood filler handy, try putting small strips of wood or wooden toothpicks in the hole and then driving the screw back into them. The screw forces the scraps of wood to take on a thread, and if the hole was not completely stripped, the scraps will blend into the sides of the hole and make a good bond.

If the hinges are tight, try to determine where the door is sticking. Some possible misalignments are shown in Figure 2-10, greatly exaggerated. In Figure 2-10(a) there is a gap near the top hinge, and the opposite edge of the door contacts the frame. If there is sufficient clearance around the door except at this point of contact, the door can be realigned by pushing it away from the frame at the bottom hinge. Remove the screws holding the bottom hinge to the frame, and insert a piece of cardboard as a shim between the hinge and the frame. This will tend to move the door slightly counterclockwise and should straighten it in the frame. In Figure 2-10(b), the gap is near the bottom hinge. This can be corrected by putting a cardboard shim under the top hinge. In Figure 2-10(c), contact is at the striker plate. Check for loose screws in both the striker and the latch. This difficulty can usually be solved by cutting deeper mortises for either the latch or striker or both.

If shimming the hinges doesn't cure the trouble, the fault may be caused by a distorted frame. If the top of the door on the latch side is rubbing against the frame, as in Figure

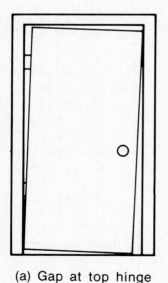 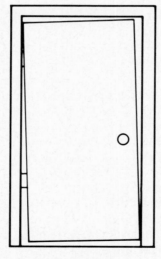 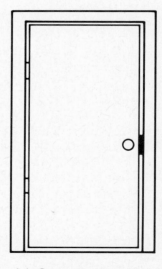

(a) Gap at top hinge   (b) Gap at bottom hinge   (c) Contact at striker

Fig. 2-10. Door misalignments.

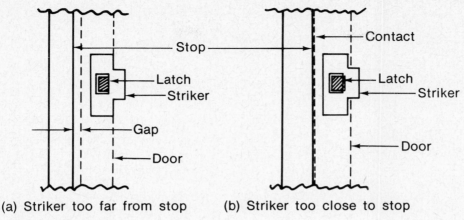

(a) Striker too far from stop   (b) Striker too close to stop

Fig. 2-11. Improper striker positions.

2-10(a), you can pull the frame back into line by driving a long nail into the opposite jamb just under the top hinge. Use a finishing nail 3″ or 4″ long, and use a nailset to drive the head below the surface. If you wish, you can cover the nailhead with putty and paint over it so it won't show, but since the nail cannot be seen when the door is closed, you don't have to be that meticulous.

If shimming a hinge causes the door to rub all along the latch edge, take out the shim and mortise the other hinge a little deeper. That is, in Figure 2-10(a), the top hinge should be mortised deeper to pull the top edge of the latch side away from its jamb.

If a door rattles when it is closed, there is too much play at the latch. This happens when the striker plate is too far from the stop on the jamb, as in Figure 2-11(a). When the latch is engaged in the striker, there is a gap between the door (shown by dotted lines) and the stop. Any slight breeze can move the door against the stop and away again, causing it to rattle. The cure is to move the striker closer to the stop. With the door closed, note the size of the gap, and then cut the mortise for the striker to move the plate about the same amount. It will be necessary to fill the old screw holes with a wood filler, and after it hardens, drill starting holes for the new positions of the screws. Otherwise, the screws would slip back into their old position and pull the striker away from the stop again.

If the striker plate is too close to the stop, as

in Figure 2-11(b), the latch will not be engaged, since it doesn't quite reach the hole. The door then will not stay closed. If only a slight shift of the plate is needed, loosen the screws slightly, pull the plate in a direction away from the stop, and insert a strip of cardboard between the edge of the striker and the edge of the mortise. Now tighten the screws, and the plate will be shifted away from the stop by the thickness of the cardboard. If a larger shift is needed, file out the opening in the striker, using a fine file, or move the striker away from the stop by filling the old screw holes with wood filler and drilling new screw holes.

If a door won't stay closed, the trouble may be caused by a vertical misalignment of the striker and latch. This happens when either the door or the frame settles. Look for marks on the striker plate which shows where the latch is hitting it. If these marks are lower than the opening (the usual case), it is necessary to lower the opening in the plate. This can be done by moving the whole plate lower on the jamb, or simply by filing the opening so that the latch is engaged.

If a door warps because of excessive moisture on one side, it can sometimes be straightened simply by drying it thoroughly. If this doesn't work, support the door with its curved side up and place heavy weights on it to force it into line. Let it stand this way for a day or two, and the door should then be usable.

3 Glass

3-1. How to Replace Glass

Replacing a broken pane in a window or door is a simple job that you can do yourself with no prior experience. You will need putty or glazier's compound and a package of glazier's points, as well as a piece of glass to fit the opening. All supplies are available in most hardware stores or in glass-supply outlets.

The first problem is to remove all pieces of the broken glass and the old putty from the frame. When you are removing the glass, wear heavy gloves of the sort sold for gardening to protect your hands from slivers. If the putty is very old and dry, it can be scraped out easily with a screwdriver or chisel. Otherwise, it may be necessary to hammer on the head of the chisel, but if you do, keep the chisel at a low angle to the wood and be careful not to gouge the frame. If the old putty is extremely hard, it can be softened by heating it with a soldering iron or torch, and then it should be easy to remove. Old glazier's points should come out with the old putty. Use pliers to pull out any points that remain.

When the frame is *clean*, a thin ribbon of putty must be placed all around the opening as a "bed" for the glass. This prevents leakage and also protects the glass from shock and vibration. However, if the putty is placed on the bare wood, the wood will tend to absorb the oil in the putty, causing the putty to dry out quickly and become brittle. To prevent this, the wood should first be coated

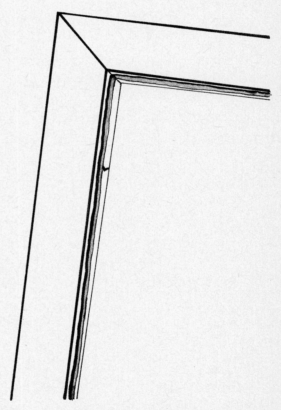

Place a ribbon of putty around opening in window frame. This acts as a "bed" for pane of glass.

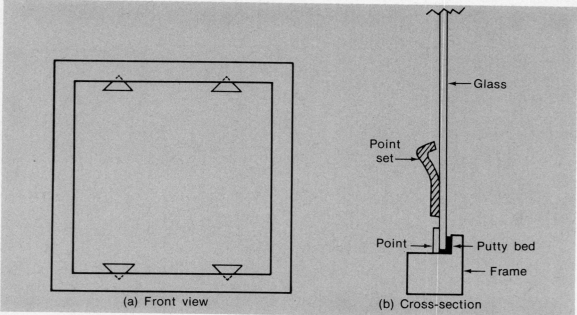

Fig. 3-1. Installing glazier's points.

with linseed oil or thinned oil-based paint. Then the bed of putty can be applied. The coating of oil saturates the wood so that it doesn't draw oil from the putty. Roll a small wad of putty between your hands to form a thin rope. Apply the putty in a thin ribbon all around the frame and press it firmly in place with the fingertips.

You can buy glass cut to size from your dealer, so it is never necessary to cut the glass yourself. Most hardware dealers will cut the glass without charge. Measure the opening accurately and order the glass about 1/8″ smaller in each dimension to allow about 1/16″ clearance on each side. If the opening is not rectangular, cut a piece of cardboard to the proper shape, and bring it to the dealer as a pattern. Press the glass carefully but firmly in place against the bed of putty, and secure it with two glazier's points on each of the four sides. *Glazier's points* are thin triangular pieces of metal. They are placed against the glass with one point of the triangle stuck firmly in the wood of the frame, as shown in Figure 3-1. A special tool called a *point set* is used to help drive in the points. This is a piece of metal which is placed over each point as it is installed, as shown in Figure 3-1(b), so that

the points can be driven in easily by hitting the top of the point set with a hammer. A point set usually comes free in each package of points,

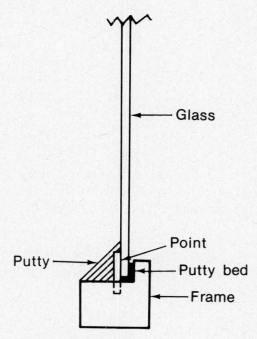

Fig. 3-2. Finished seal.

but if you don't have one, you can use a screwdriver instead. While you are hitting the tool with a hammer, the head of the hammer remains in contact with the glass at all times.

Add a few more glazier's points about every 4″ or 5″ all around the edges of the glass to hold the glass in place before applying the final layer of putty. This final seal is also applied with the fingertips, but it is then smoothed with a putty knife at an angle, as shown in Figure 3-2, which illustrates the cross section of a complete putty seal. Any excess putty is removed with the putty knife. Note that the *points* hold the glass in place; the putty merely prevents leaks. After the putty is smoothed, you can apply an oil-based paint over it immediately. This paint layer harmonizes with the window trim, but more importantly, it keeps the putty from drying out.

Panes for metal windows are installed in the same manner, except that special spring clips are used to hold the glass instead of glazier's points. These clips fit into holes in the metal frames. Remove the old putty, being careful to save the clips. Clean the frame and lay a bed of putty. Press in the glass and hold it, with the clips inserted in the same holes as before. Put on a final layer of putty and seal it with paint. For metal windows you should use double-strength glass.

3-2. Sash Cords

A window sash is balanced by weights attached to sash cords. When a sash cord breaks or a weight slips off the end of a cord, the window is no longer counterbalanced and tends to fall when raised. You can keep the window open, if necessary, by propping it up with a piece of wood, but sooner or later you will want to replace the cord. This is a simple job, once you have solved the mystery of how to get at the cord. Figure 3-3 shows the window tracks in a common double-hung window, as well as the stops and other parts of the window frame. The upper sash moves in the outside track, and the lower in the inside. The two tracks are separated by a *parting*

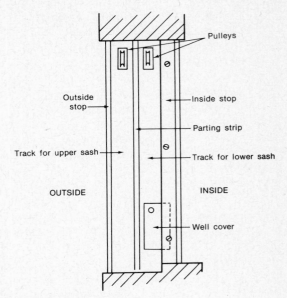

Fig. 3-3. Window tracks.

strip, which is held in a slot between the tracks by friction. Pulleys at the top of each track support the sash cords. Counterweights attached to the cords move up and down in a deep well behind the tracks as the windows are lowered or raised.

Figure 3-4 shows how a sash cord is attached to a window. A knot on the end of the cord fits into a socket or large indentation in the side of the sash. The rope above the knot lies in a groove along the side of the window, but the groove is too narrow for the knot to slip through. The sash cord passes over its pulley at the top of the track and is attached to a weight. Each window sash has two weights supporting it, and ideally the sum of the weights of the two counterweights should equal the weight of the sash, although friction between the tracks and the sash permits some deviation from this ideal. When a sash is all the way down, its counterweights should be near the top of the well. When the sash is fully raised, the weights should not touch the bottom of the well.

To replace a broken sash cord, it is necessary to remove the sash. For an upper sash, it is necessary to remove the lower sash as well. The first step is to remove the inside stop. Remove the screws holding it to the frame (refer to Figure 3-3), and pry the stop loose with a screwdriver or an old chisel. The first time this is done, you will break the paint seal between the stop and the frame. After that, it will be easy to remove the stop. With one stop removed, you can lift out the lower sash. It is not necessary to remove the stop on the other side unless you are going to replace both sash cords attached to the one sash. With the sash removed, you can get at the well cover. One or two screws must be removed, and then the well cover can be pried off, revealing the weights inside the well. Pass a new rope over the pulley and attach the inside end to its proper weight. Tie a knot in the outside end (Figure 3-4), and push the knot into the socket on the side of the sash. Put the window back in its tracks and replace the inside stop. When the knot is placed in the socket and the sash is near its bottom position, the rope should be cut to the proper length so that the weight is near the pulley. Buy *soft* rope specially for sash cords.

For a top sash, you must remove the bottom sash as described above and also pull out one parting strip. Then the top sash can be removed, and the cord replaced as described

above. When the bottom sash is removed to get at the top sash, it is necessary to remove the cords from the bottom sash. Just pull the knots out of their sockets, but be careful not to let go of the ropes suddenly. Holding the knot, let the weight pull the rope until the knot is next to the pulley. Then it is safe to release the knot, since it won't slip past the pulley.

3-3. Stuck Windows

When a double-hung window is stuck and cannot be opened, the trouble is due either to dampness which caused the sash to swell or to paint that has been applied improperly and has sealed the window to its stop. Freeing a stuck window is not a difficult task, but the methods used depend to some extent on the cause.

If a sash is stuck because paint has hardened, joining the sash to a stop or to the sill, it is necessary to break the paint seal. Use a putty knife, if you have one, or any other thin blade, and insert it between the sash and the stop. Tap the blade lightly with a hammer, and simply cut the paint. Alternatively, you can force an old chisel or a hatchet blade between the bottom of the window and the frame from outside. As you tap on the back of the hatchet or the handle of the chisel, the taper forces the window open, breaking the paint seal. Once the window has moved, it usually can be opened easily. Scrape away the extra paint so that the window will not jam again when it is closed. If you wish, you can sand the edge to make it smooth. If none of these methods is effective, you must remove the inside stop and free the window in the same manner described in Section 3-2 for replacing a sash cord. Pry off the stop carefully, since you will be breaking the paint seal as you do.

When a sash sticks because of dampness, you can sometimes loosen the window by hammering the stop away from the sash. Use a small block of wood between the hammerhead and the stop so that you do not mar the stop. Again, if this doesn't work, you can free the window by removing the inside stops and

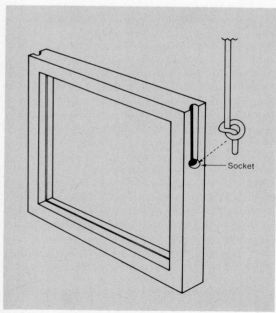

Fig. 3-4. Sash and cord.

the sash. If the sash moves stiffly without the stop in place, it indicates that the sash itself is swollen. Remove the sash, and plane or sand the edge so that it moves freely. Before putting it back, rub the edge with paraffin or wax. This lubricates the sash so that it slides better and also forms a seal against moisture.

When steel casement windows are difficult to move, the trouble may be due to excessive paint but is most often caused by inadequate lubrication. Oil all moving parts at the first sign of sticking. Sand off any rust spots, and touch up with a rust-resistant primer. Break paint seals by moving the window back and forth a few times, and scrape away any accumulated layers of paint.

The tracks of sliding doors and windows may be kept lubricated with silicone pray.

4 Stairs

If a flight of stairs is rickety and needs strengthening, call a professional carpenter. However, there are some minor stair repairs you can do yourself, and if you take care of your stairs, you will never need a major repair job.

4-1. Construction of Stairs

A cross-sectional view of part of a flight of stairs is shown in Figure 4-1. The steps are supported on two long beams called stringers, one on either side of the flight. On very wide steps, a third stringer may be used in the middle. The stringers have cut out spaces for the treads and risers. The treads and risers are nailed to the stringers and also nailed to each other. In the figure, the top riser is shown with a tongue-and-groove joint to the two treads it joins. The other joints shown are simple butt joints. In practice, a flight of stairs will have all the joints of one variety, but both are shown in the figure for illustrative purposes. The tongue-and-groove joint is usually glued and nailed and is thus somewhat stronger than the butt joint, which is only nailed. A decorative molding, as shown under the nose of one tread, is sometimes added.

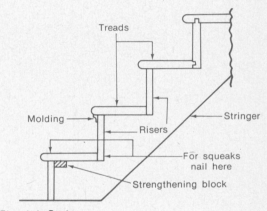

Fig. 4-1. Stairs.

4-2. Squeaky Stairs

When stairs squeak as you walk on them, the noise is caused by a loosened tread rubbing against a riser or against one of the stringers. You can stop the squeak by squirting a lubricating powder into the crack between the tread and riser, but this is only a temporary solution. Solve the problem completely by nailing the tread firmly to the risers. If you can get under the stairs, also nail the risers to the treads (see the bottom tread in Figure 4-1).

4-3. Replacing Treads

A well-maintained staircase is not only safe, but also attractive.

Use finishing nails, 2″ or 3″ long, and space them about 3″ apart. For best results, drive the nails at an angle and in alternate directions so that they are not holding the same way. For an additional bond, nail and glue a small block of wood under the stairs at the junction of a tread and riser, as shown under the bottom tread in the figure. Countersink any nailheads on the surface of the stairs and fill the hole with putty colored to match the coating on the stairs.

Constant use wears the treads, and you may decide to replace them. If the treads and risers are connected with butt joints it is a simple matter to pry up the treads and turn them over. Of course, if someone has already done this, the bottom side will be too worn also, and then you must get new treads. If the nails holding the treads are set at angles, as they should be, you may find it difficult to pull the tread up off the riser. Use a small all-purpose saw between the tread and riser to cut all the nails. Then when the tread is off, you can drive out the nails if you intend to reverse the tread and use it again. If the treads have decorative moldings, pry off the moldings before trying to remove the treads.

For treads joined to risers by a tongue-and-groove joint, saw off the tongue as you saw the nails. When you reverse the tread, fill the groove on the bottom side with wood filler, and paint over it. Don't worry about not having tongue-and-groove joints. Most stairs do not have them.

If looks are not too important, on cellar stairs for example, you can simply cover worn treads with sheets of 1/2″ plywood cut to the size of the tread. Nail the plywood to the top of the tread. A similar approach, but more decorative, is to use tiles or linoleum as a cover. To do this, first fill in depressions on the tread with floor filler, and then cement the linoleum or tiles on top. An ornamental molding or metal strip can be placed along the nose (front) of each tread to hide the seam between the linoleum and the wood.

Before improving a staircase, tighten loose treads and risers as described in Section 4—2.

5

Floors

5-1. Wood Floors

The common wood floor used in most houses consists of two layers. The subfloor is a layer of flat boards nailed directly on the large supporting joists. These boards usually are laid at an angle of 45° to the joists, although in some cases they are laid at right angles. The floor itself is made of tongue-and-groove flooring, as shown in Figure 1-2(a), and repeated here in Figure 5-1. Each board has a tongue along one edge and a groove on the opposite edge. In addition, the opposite ends of the boards may also have a tongue

and a groove, respectively. Where the subfloor is laid at an angle of 45° to the joists, the top layer is 90° or at right angles to the joists. If the subfloor is at right angles to the joists, the top layer is usually parallel to the joists. A layer of building paper is placed between the two layers of flooring for insulation and to provide a resilient surface to take care of imperfections in the flooring. In Figure 5-1, a small space is shown at the bottom of each seam. This space ensures that at floor level the boards will make good contact and provide a continuous surface without cracks. However, the angle is barely discernible, and on some softwood floorboards, it may be omitted.

One advantage of tongue-and-groove flooring is that it permits invisible nailing. The groove of each board is fitted to the tongue of the preceding board. Nails are placed along the tongue at an angle (Figure 5-2). Each nail

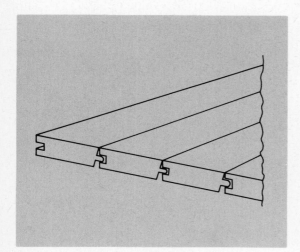

Fig. 5-1. Tongue-and-groove flooring.

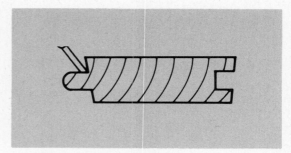

Fig. 5-2. Nailing flooring.

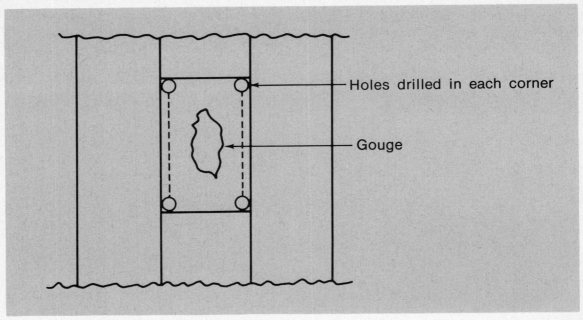

Fig. 5-3. Removing damaged section of flooring.

is countersunk with a nailset so as not to interfere with the fit between the tongue and groove of the next board. There are special flooring nails, but any kind of small-headed or headless nails can be used. For floorboards about 3/4″ thick, the nails should be about 2-1/2″ long and spaced every 10″ or 12″ along the tongue.

If a small section of the top flooring is gouged or otherwise damaged, you can replace it. First mark it off carefully and then drill a large hole in each corner (Figure 5-3). These holes should not penetrate the sub-floor. With a chisel, split the section by cutting from hole to hole along the grain, as indicated by the dotted lines in the figure. Cut across the grain at the ends. Remove the damaged section by literally chopping it up with the chisel. Be careful not to damage the adjacent tongue and groove. A new board is cut to length to fit in the opening. The underside of the groove must be removed (Figure 5-4), to get it into the space. For best results, plane off the bottom edge of the groove, but if you are careful, you can remove it with a chisel. Drill a pilot hole for a finishing nail in each corner of the new section and drive in the nails. Without

pilot holes the nails could split the wood. Countersink the nails and cover heads with wood filler.

A squeak in a floor indicates a space between the joist and subfloor or between the subfloor and top floor. If you can get under the floor, look for such a space between the joist and subfloor. This can be caused by a sagging joist or a loose nail in the subfloor. To cure the problem, wedge a thin piece of wood into the space. To keep the wedge firm, coat it with glue before inserting it. If the subfloor is firmly attached to the joist, but the top floor seems to move slightly on it, pull the top floor down to the subfloor, by inserting screws from below. Allowing about 3/4 inch for each of the two floor layers, the screws should be at least 1″ long and not more than 1-1/4″.

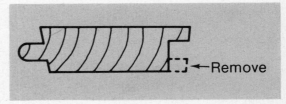

Fig. 5-4. Cross-section of replacement section.

If you cannot get under the floor because there is a ceiling below it, drive nails into the floor itself to fasten it down. First, locate the joists. To do this, place a small block of hardwood on the floor and tap it with a hammer. When the block is over a joist, there is a "solid" sound when you hammer on it. Between joists there is a hollow thud. Joists are 16" apart, so when you locate one, you should have no difficulty in finding the rest. The block prevents damaging the floor with the hammer. After locating a joist, drive nails into the floor at the joist at an angle, alternating the angle at adjacent nails. Use 2-1/2" or longer finishing nails or threaded flooring nails. If the squeak is between joists, indicating a space between the floor and subfloor, drive nails at an angle at the point of the squeak to push the top floor down. In all cases, countersink the nails with a nailset so that the heads are below the surface of the floor. Use a wood filler to hide the nailheads.

In an old house, floors may sag noticeably. This may be caused by the shrinkage of joists or other supporting members or by a gradual sinking into the ground. If there is a sag on the first floor of the house, it can usually be corrected easily by using a jack post to prop up the supporting timber. Jack posts look like oversized automobile jacks and are available at building suppliers. Some special tools are needed to install a jack post, but they are inexpensive. At the point on the basement floor directly below the beam to be supported, attach a base plate to prevent the jack post from moving sideways. You will need a star drill or a masonry bit to make holes in the cement or concrete in the basement; these are described in Section 1-7. Make holes at least 1" deep for the bolts to hold down the metal base plate. Use the plate itself as a template to locate the positions of the holes. Lead expansion anchors are placed in the holes. These expand when bolts are driven into them, and the pressure holds the bolts in place.

The jack is set on the base plate and extended until its top plate just touches the timber to be supported. Use a level to make certain that the post is vertical. Then fasten the top plate to the timber with nails or screws to prevent slipping. Turn the screw on the jack post about one quarter turn and let it set for a day. Then turn it up *only one half turn per week*, until the sag is not noticeable. If you try to jack up the beam faster than this you can damage the house frame and even break gas or water pipes. When you move in small increments, everything in the house stretches or settles between movements to adjust to the small pressure.

5-2. How to Install a New Threshold

When a threshold is so worn that there is a visible gap under the door, even with weather stripping in place, it is time to replace the threshold. The first and hardest part of the job is removing the old threshold. Installing a new one is relatively simple.

It is best to remove the door to give yourself as much room as possible to get out the old threshold. Simply remove the pins in the hinges and lift the door out. To remove a pin, hold a wooden rod or an old screwdriver under the head of the pin, and hit it gently with a hammer. If the pin is stuck, drive it out with a punch through the hole in the bottom of the hinge. After the door is removed, pry off the door stop on both side jambs. Use an old chisel and pry off in small increments so as not to crack the stop. If you do split a stop, you can glue the pieces together again.

When the stops are out, you may be able to remove the old threshold in one piece. Slide it out if it protrudes under the jambs. If it cannot be removed, split it with a chisel to simplify removal. Use the old threshold as a pattern for a new one, if possible. If it is too badly damaged, measure the space for a new one. The new one should look something like the one shown in Figure 5-5. Slide the new one under the jambs and into position. If you are replacing the threshold on an outside door, you should put a layer of roofing asphalt or linoleum cement under the threshold to make a waterproof and windproof seal.

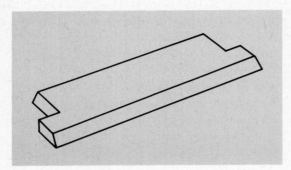

Fig. 5-5. Threshold.

If you cannot slide the new threshold under the jambs because it is thicker than the old or the floor is uneven, cut scraps of wood to fit the spaces under the jambs. Then fit the new threshold flush with the jambs instead of under them. Similarly, if you cannot slide out the old threshold, you can cut it off flush with the jambs, using a small handsaw. Then fit a new threshold into the space.

The new threshold should be made of hardwood for long wear. This makes it harder to nail down. Use pilot holes about 1/16" in diameter through the threshold to avoid splitting the wood, and nail it in place with 2" or 2-1/2" finishing nails. Countersink the nailheads with a nailset and cover the heads with wood filler.

5-3. How to Refinish Wood Floors

When a floor has a few scratches in it, you can usually remove the damage without having to resort to a complete refinishing. If the scratches do not penetrate farther than the finish, they can be removed with steel wool. If there are stains as well as scratches, use a cleaning agent with the steel wool. Rub only in the direction of the grain. When the scratched finish is removed, smooth the surface with fine sandpaper or fine steel wool, and apply a matching shellac or varnish. Dilute shellac slightly with alcohol, dilute varnish with turpentine.

If scratches are deep and penetrate the floor, remove the finish, as indicated above, and smooth the wood. Then fill the scratches with wood filler or wood plastic to a level above the surface of the floor. Remove excess with a putty knife. When it is dry, sand it flush with the floor, using smooth sandpaper. Finish with shellac or varnish as above.

Refinishing a floor completely is not a difficult job, but it requires special equipment, which can usually be rented. There are three steps in refinishing: (1) sanding off the old finish; (2) applying a finishing coat of varnish or shellac; and (3) applying a coat of wax to protect the finish.

Before beginning to sand, remove all furniture from the room, including pictures, drapes and Venetian blinds. Sanding leaves a thin layer of dust on everything. Look carefully over the floor and if you see any nailheads, drive them down with a nailset. This is a good time also to nail down any loose boards or squeaky spots in the floor. Open the windows, shut the doors, and you are ready to begin.

You will need to rent a drum sander and a disc sander. The drum sander is used first to cover all large areas in the room. Sand parallel to the grain. Follow the directions supplied with the machine, and you will find it simple to operate. The disc sander is for edges not accessible with the larger drum sander. With both sanders, you can begin with a coarse paper to remove the finish and then progress to finer sandpaper in a second and third operation.

After sanding, and before beginning the finishing, go over the *whole room* with a vacuum cleaner, including tops of doors, windows, and baseboards. Any dust left in the room can spoil the finish.

Finishes for floors are in three categories. *Floor sealers* soak into the wood and do not form a film or coating on the surface. *Varnishes, shellacs* and some *synthetic* finishes form a surface coating which may be colored but is usually transparent so that the wood grain is visible. Floor *paints* cover the floor with an opaque coating. The choice depends on the type of finish desired.

If you want a matte finish, use a floor sealer. Apply the first coat with a brush or mop, or

The edges of a new door may be planed if the door doesn't fit properly.

wipe it on with a cloth. If you wish to add color to the floor, you can get colored sealer. Let the sealer remain on the floor for about 15 or 20 minutes, and then wipe off the excess. Let it dry overnight, then rent an electric buffer and go over the floor. Now add a second sealer in the same way. The sealer finish is usually scratchproof. Worn areas can be touched up simply by wiping on more sealer, with no danger of lap marks showing.

Varnish makes a pleasing finish, but it is slow drying and therefore awkward to use. So-called "quick-drying" varnishes should not be used, since they are not durable. Varnish can be put down over an old finish if the old finish is in good condition. For new wood or resanded wood, use a sealer for the first coat. After it has dried overnight, apply the varnish. You should put on at least two coats of varnish, waiting at least 24 hours for each coat to dry. Alternatively, you can use a coat of thinned shellac as a sealer, and then two coats of varnish. Allow each coat to dry thoroughly before applying the next. A varnish finish darkens with age.

Shellac is simple to apply and dries quickly. White shellac does not stain wood, so the natural grain is visible. Orange shellac also shows the grain but darkens the wood somewhat. Shellac should be applied in thin coats. Shellac as purchased should be thinned with alcohol. Ask your paint dealer to advise you how much to thin it, since dealers may mix their own shellac already thinned. For bare wood, plan on using three coats of shellac, allowing each coat to dry at least two hours before applying the next. Shellac is not as water-resistant as varnish, but is easier to apply, and worn areas can be touched up easily.

Synthetic or plastic finishes are the most durable. They *require no wax* and will last for years. They must be thinned with a special thinner and can then be brushed on easily. Two coats are enough. These materials are available in either a glossy or matte finish.

When your final finish is dry, you should wax the floor to protect the finish. Do not use a self-polishing liquid wax on a wood floor because they contain too much water, which can damage wood. Paste wax and solvent-based liquid waxes (not self-polishing) are satisfactory. Apply with a soft cloth and let dry about 20 or 30 minutes. Then use the electric buffer to polish. Two thin coats, buffed separately, give a longer-lasting shine than one thick coat.

5-4. How to Lay a Wood Floor over Concrete

If you want to convert a basement room or a garage for "living" quarters, you may wish to have a wood floor laid over the concrete floor already there. You can do it yourself. The most important step is to make sure you have a good vapor barrier under the floor. Waterproof mastic is excellent. Spread it liberally over the concrete with a trowel or other flat-faced tool. A putty knife will do in a pinch. The mastic prevents moisture in the concrete from reaching the wood, where it can cause the floor to shrink or warp.

You will not need a subfloor, but you will need *screeds* on which to nail the floorboards. Screeds are short sections of 2 × 4's, pressed right into the mastic and lapped (Figure 5-6). The rows should be about 1' apart, and the overlap between screeds should be about 4" or 5". The length of a screed is not critical; anything up to about 3' is satisfactory.

Tongue-and-groove flooring is laid perpendicular to the screeds. It is usually a good idea to buy the flooring as much as a week in advance and store it in a dry, warm place in your home. This will tend to remove any excessive moisture in the wood. Nail only on the tongue side of the board, as shown in Figure 5-2 and described in Section 5-1. Nail each board to every screed it crosses. This not only makes the floor stronger but also holds the screeds together. After every three or four courses are laid (a course is one board or one line all across the room), place a scrap of flooring with its groove against the tongue of the last course, and hit the scrap with a hammer to drive the courses together.

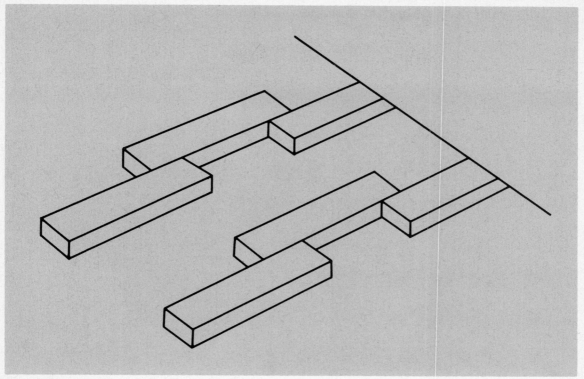

Fig. 5-6. Screeds.

When you get close to the opposite wall, you won't have enough room to drive nails into the tongue at an angle. You will have to drive nails into the face of the flooring. Make sure that you know the location of the screeds so that you nail the floorboards to them. It is best to drill pilot holes 1/16" in diameter in the floorboards before driving nails in the face, since hardwoods can be split by nailing. When the flooring is all laid, nail a shoe molding around the room to hide cracks between the walls and the floor.

5-5. How to Lay Flexible Tiles

Tiling a floor is a boring but simple job. Flexible tiles are available in vinyl, asbestos, cork, rubber, linoleum, asphalt and combinations of these materials. For durability, vinyl tiles are best, or some combination of vinyl such as vinyl-asphalt or vinyl-asbestos. Use some form of vinyl tile in areas where you expect a lot of traffic. Linoleum, rubber and asphalt are all grease-resistant, and, therefore, one of these should be selected for kitchens and other cooking areas. Cork is attractive but the least durable.

Most tiles are available in 9" × 9" squares. Occasionally, you may find 12" × 12", 9" × 18", and other odd sizes. With 9" × 9" tiles, figure on buying two tiles per square foot of area in your room. With 12" × 12" or 9" × 18", buy 11 tiles for every 10 square feet. The extra tiles are necessary because room dimensions are not usually divisible by tile sizes, and you must make allowance for some waste. In very large areas, there will be much less waste than in small rooms.

No matter what kind of tiles you put down, the first step is to prepare the floor. Remember that any irregularities in the floor will show up in the tiles. If you are putting the tiles on a wood floor in good condition, just check that

Regardless of what type of heating system you have, it is important to keep a check on gauges, ducts, and pipes.

How to hang wallpaper. See page 57 of this volume.

no nailheads are protruding. Countersink any visible nails. If the floor has small irregularities, sand or plane them smooth. Before laying the tiles, sweep the floor clean.

If tiles are to be laid on a concrete floor, the concrete should not be painted, nor have any cracks. Fill cracks with any filler material that sets hard. If the concrete has a coat of paint, you have to cover it with an underlayment of thin plywood or hardboard panels. Cover the concrete floor with a layer of waterproof mastic as a vapor barrier, and press the underlayment into the mastic. Joints in the underlayment should have cracks about 1/32″ wide to allow for expansion of the material. The tiles will be placed to cover the cracks. Clean the floor before applying tiles.

If the wood floor on which the tiles will be laid is rough or irregular, you should use an underlayment of plywood or hardboard sheets. Leave 1/32″ cracks between adjacent sheets to allow for expansion. Nail the underlayment to the wooden floor. Sweep clean before laying the tiles.

The best way to plan how to lay the tiles is to use squared paper with each square representing a tile. You may want all the tiles the same color, or you may want a pattern. Use colored pencils or crayons to plan the floor on paper first.

Find the center of the room. To do this, measure the center points on two opposite walls, and connect them with a chalk line. Do the same with the other two walls. The center of the room is where the chalk lines intersect. Lay out two crossing rows of tiles along the chalk lines from the center to the walls. These are not cemented down but are put down as a kind of first fitting. The space between the wall and the tile nearest it should be at least 2″. If necessary, move the chalk lines so that there is no space smaller than this.

Beginning at the chalk line, coat half the room with mastic or adhesive. A special adhesive is needed on concrete floors. Also, a special adhesive is needed with asphalt tiles. Follow the instructions on the can. Some adhesives must be allowed to dry before applying the tile. The adhesive is spread with a special grooved trowel (Figure 5-7). When the mastic is tacky (or as indicated in the instructions), start to lay the tile. Do not slide the tiles to their positions, but try to place them correctly the first time. Put the first tile with its edges along the two chalk lines. Then place tiles next to three sides of the first tile. Continue, placing each new tile next to a tile already down until half the room is covered, except for the small space next to the wall. Then cover the other half of the room in the same manner. You will have to cut tiles to make them fit in the smaller spaces next to the wall. First mark the tile to be cut (Figure 5-8). One tile is placed exactly over the tile laid nearest the wall. This is tile A in the figure. A second tile, B in the figure, is placed with its

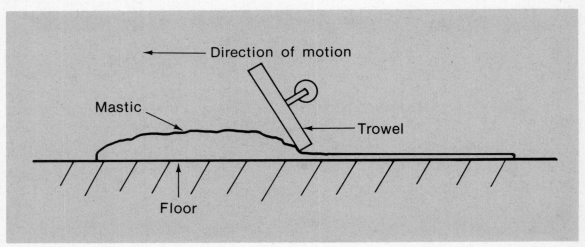

Fig. 5-7. Applying mastic.

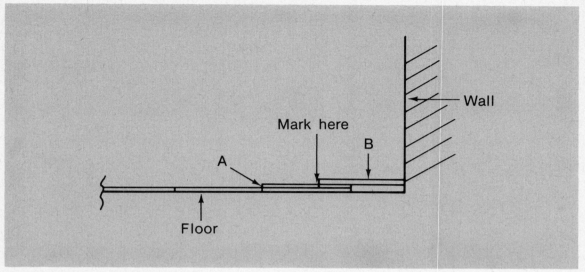

Fig. 5-8. Marking tile for cutting.

edge against the wall and is used as a guide to make a line on A. Cut tile A on the line, and the piece cut off will fit the space exactly. Most tiles can be cut with ordinary scissors or a linoleum knife. Tiles are easier to cut if the temperature is above 70° F. Asphalt tiles must be scored, and then can be snapped along the scored line.

You need a few special tools to lay tiles or linoleum, including a special trowel, a linoleum knife, and chalk lines. You may buy these in an inexpensive kit, with complete instructions, from mail-order houses and most building-supply stores.

Some vinyl-asbestos tiles are available with an adhesive backing; these are simple to install. After the floor is prepared, just peel the backing off and press the tile in place. No mastic is necessary. The adhesive will stick to concrete as well as to wood.

When one or more tiles in a tile floor are damaged, pry them loose and replace them with new ones. To remove an old tile, heat it by putting an iron on it for a few seconds. This softens the old mastic. Use a linoleum knife to pry out the old tile. If the old mastic is tacky, you don't have to apply new mastic. Just put your new tile in place, and it will stick. If the old mastic is dry, scrape it out, and add new mastic before laying the new tile.

5-6. How to Lay Linoleum

Linoleum is available in the form of tiles, in strips and in room-sized pieces. The same general rules for floor preparations as were discussed in Section 5-5 apply here. Make sure the floor is clean. Linoleum can be laid on top of an old worn linoleum if the old layer is not chopped up.

As with tiles, a paste is spread first and the linoleum laid on that. Sometimes the paste can be omitted when laying a linoleum covering in one large piece, but if two or more pieces are used, you must use paste especially where the pieces join.

If an old linoleum has a worn-out spot, you can replace just the spot without having to replace the whole covering. Cut out the worn section with a linoleum knife or scissors, and cut an exact piece to fit. Use the old section as pattern. If the new linoleum is thinner than the old, use newspaper to shim it up. Apply paste to both sides of the paper, or if no paper is used, apply the paste to the floor. Press the patch into position. Hold it down with weights until the cement dries. If edges are uneven, hammer them down or sand them.

Use a large putty knife to apply spackling compound to hairline cracks.

5-7. How to Lay Ceramic Tiles

At one time, laying ceramic tiles was a job for a professional, but manufacturers with an eye on the do-it-yourself market have simplified procedures. With special adhesives and even adhesive-backed tiles, you can lay ceramic tiles as easily as the flexible tiles described in Section 5-6. The floor must be smooth and clean. Follow the manufacturer's instructions for applying the adhesive and the tiles. Ceramic tile floors are more expensive than other materials, but they last indefinitely and require almost no maintenance.

One form of ceramic tile is an arrangement of very small tiles, usually referred to as *mosaic*. A mosaic floor is easy to put down. The tiles are furnished with their faces stuck on a piece of paper about 1 foot square. The "square" as it is called, is put down as one unit on the mastic, which has been spread on the floor. First, the square is placed with the paper side up, and after the mastic has dried, the paper is washed off by soaking it with water. The mosaic tiles are spaced on the paper, and squares are put down with similar spaces between adjacent tiles. These spaces must be filled with grout. Simply push it into the joints with a trowel or putty knife, and after a few minutes wipe off the excess.

A tile entryway is both pleasing and functional, since this portion of the house gets a lot of traffic. If the front door of your house opens into a large hallway, you might consider putting a tile floor over the first 6' or 8' from the door. You can begin right at the threshold, or you can lift the threshold first and have the tile begin under the threshold. Then the threshold is replaced and conceals the joint between the tiles and the wood floor (Figure 5-9). You may have to plane off part of the underside of the threshold to keep it from interfering with the door.

As with other tiles, kits are available that contain all the necessary tools and complete instructions. A kit costs little compared to the cost of the materials and is well worth buying when you undertake this job.

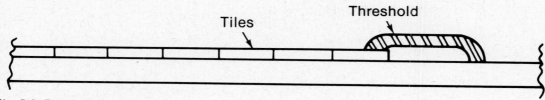

Fig. 5-9. Threshold covering joint.

Walls and Ceilings

6-1. Wall Finishes

At one time, most interior walls and ceilings were made of plaster and covered with paint or wallpaper. Although plaster is cheap, it is not a good material, since it absorbs moisture. When temperatures rise, the water in the plaster evaporates back into the room where it can be harmful to finishes on walls, floor and furniture. If you have plaster walls, however, you should not replace them as long as they are in good condition. You can repair cracks and dents in plaster walls easily. If you are planning a *new* wall or partition, do not use plaster.

Modern wall finishes include plywood, wood panelling, fiberboard, plasterboard, wallboard, plastics, tiles and many others. The characteristics of some of the many wall surfaces are given in Table 6-1. Remember that the characteristics shown apply to the bare materials. When the wall is covered with paint, paper or tiles, it is much easier to clean and resists moisture better than the bare material. Hardboard is available with many different decorative finishes, including simulated leather, wood panelling and painted surfaces in a variety of colors. All the material can be used on ceilings as well as walls.

If you plan to cover the wall with paint, wallpaper, tiles or linoleum, your best bet for

Table 6-1. Characteristics of Wall Materials

Material	Moisture Resistance	Ease in Application	Ease in Cleaning	Durability
Unfinished plywood	Fair	Easy	Difficult	Good
Finished plywood	Fair	Easy	Easy	Good
Bare plaster	Poor	Difficult	Difficult	Poor
Fiberboard	Fair	Easy	Difficult	Fair
Gypsum wallboard	Fair	Easy	Difficult	Good
Plasterboard	Poor	Easy	Difficult	Fair
Plastic sheets	Excellent	Moderate	Easy	Excellent
Hardboard	Excellent	Easy	Easy	Excellent

the base is unfinished plywood. A good second choice is gypsum wallboard.

6-2. How to Patch Plaster

Holes in plaster, from small cracks to openings large enough to put your hand through, are usually repaired with spackling compound. This comes in powder form and is mixed with water as needed to make a smooth paste. The ratio of powder is not critical. The paste must be smooth — but stiff enough to remain where it is spread without running, and soft enough to spread easily. Spackling compound in paste form, that is, already mixed, is also available.

Before applying the spackling paste to the job, wet the plaster around the hole or on both sides of the crack with a sponge or damp cloth. Plaster tends to absorb moisture, and if the spackling compound is placed on dry plaster, the moisture from the compound will be drawn out too rapidly to make a good bond.

For small holes or hairline cracks, apply the spackling compound to the spot to be filled with a large putty knife. Use only a little more compound than is necessary to fill the opening, and smooth it to a feather edge, removing any excess with the putty knife. For larger openings, first scrape away any loose plaster in the crack. Use a screwdriver, beer can opener or any pointed tool to do this. To make a good bond, it is generally supposed that the crack should be wider inside the wall than at the surface, as in Figure 6-1(a). However, ideally the crack should be undercut on both sides, as in Figure 6-1(b). Practically, it doesn't make too much difference. Open the crack wide enough to clean out all loose plaster, and then apply the spackle. If the opening is large, allow a first coat to dry and then apply a second. When the job is finished, the wall can be covered with paint, wallpaper or whatever you wish.

If there is a lot of loose plaster, chisel away any edges which arouse the least suspicion of fault. If you cut away too much, you can patch

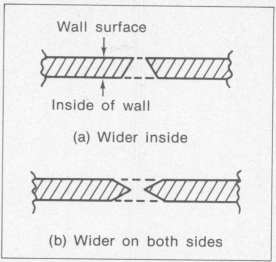

Fig. 6-1. Undercutting crack in plaster.

up the hole, but if you leave some crumbly plaster, the whole job will be spoiled later.

When a large opening is to be plastered over, as when an electric fixture is removed, you will have to furnish a base for the spackling compound. One way to do this is to cut a piece of plasterboard to fit into the opening and nail it to the studs or joists behind the plaster. When it is in place, the plasterboard should be about 1/8″ below the outer surface of the plaster. Now you need only a 1/8″ layer of spackling compound to finish the job. If you do not have any plasterboard or similar material, you can do an adequate job by stuffing the hole with newspaper crammed in about 1/8″ below the plaster surface. Then finish with spackling compound as before.

6-3. How to Build a Wall

Building a wall to divide a large room in two or to wall in a basement playroom is not as difficult as it might seem. Such a wall has no structural importance, since it does not have to support anything above it, and thus it can be quite simple. Before starting the job, you will have to plan it thoroughly, however, being

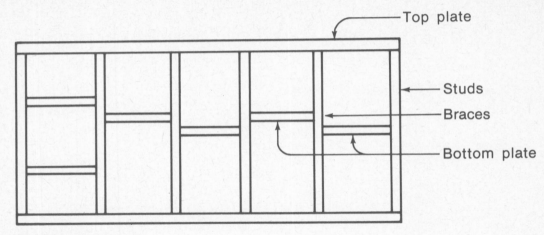

Fig. 6-2. Framework for wall.

certain to take into consideration such things as ventilation, light, heat and possibly plumbing.

First, you must build a framework, as shown in Figure 6-2. The lumber in the framework can be 2″ × 3″ stock joined with 3″ nails. Begin by nailing the bottom plate to the floor from wall to wall. If the floor is wooden, nail the plate to the floor with nails every 20 to 24 inches. If the floor is concrete, you will have to drill holes in the plate and the concrete and insert special plugs, and then screw the plate to the concrete. Since many different types of fasteners for this purpose are available, ask your hardware or building-supply dealer to recommend a kind he carries and to tell you what size of holes to drill. If you plan a doorway in the new wall, do not drive any nails or other fasteners into the plate where the door will be located.

The top plate is fastened to the ceiling next. It must be placed directly over the bottom plate. You can use a plumb line to locate it accurately or a straight board and a level. The top plate should be perpendicular to the joists above, and it can be nailed directly on to the joists. If you must run the wall parallel to the joists, you should locate the top plate directly on a joist. In this case, put up the top plate first, and place the bottom plate directly below it. This may mean moving the location

of the wall a few inches from your original plan. Studs are added next. They should be cut to length to fit between the plates. The studs at each end are flush with the side walls. All studs are toenailed to the plates from both sides. Use nails about 2-1/2″ long. In standard construction, studs are usually spaced 16″ apart between centers, but since this is merely a partition, it is quite all right to have larger spaces, even up to 2′. Short lengths of 2″ × 3″ stock are cut to fit between studs as braces. Note that in Figure 6-2 these are staggered so that nails can be driven through the studs into the braces. For most walls you should use two braces between adjacent studs, as shown between the two studs at the left of the figure. However, for lightweight wall coverings, a single brace between adjacent studs is sufficient.

If you lay out and plan your work accurately, you can cut the braces first and use them to locate the position of each stud from the preceding one. This eliminates the need to worry about positioning the stud exactly vertical.

If you plan a doorway, the framework must have an opening for the door, as shown in Figure 6-3. In this case the end studs are placed first and then the studs on each side of the doorway. Allow 1-3/4″ on each side for the rough doorway framework plus an addi-

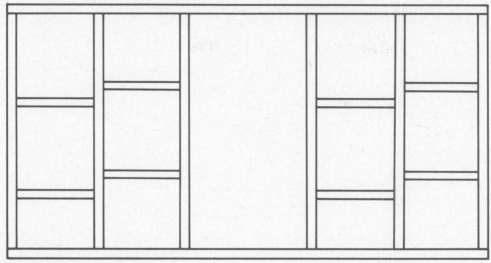

Fig. 6-3. Framework with doorway.

tional 1″ on each side and top for the door frame, if a frame is to be used.

The doorway itself is shown in Figure 6-4. First, cut out the bottom plate with a saw between the studs on each side of the doorway. Nail a shorter stud to the studs on each side. These shorter studs extend from the floor to the height of the doorway. Be sure to nail them onto the floor plate as well as onto the studs. In the figure, you will note two boards above the doorway. These are two 2″ × 3″ nailed together to form a lintel. A short piece 2″ × 3″ is added between the lintel and the ceiling plate. If the door will have a threshold, don't forget to consider the thickness of the threshold in planning the height of the door.

If the wall will have other openings, as for windows, they are surrounded by double thicknesses of 2″ × 3″ stock in the same manner. Short sections of 2″ × 3″ stock are

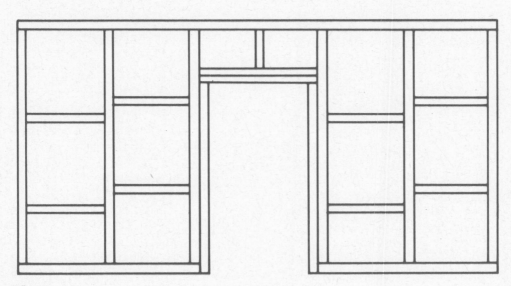

Fig. 6-4. Doorway.

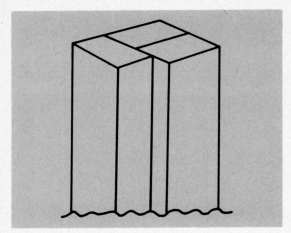

Fig. 6-5. Corner post.

floor and ceiling. This is usually done with some kind of molding nailed along the joint. At floor level, a simple baseboard nailed along the wall may be sufficient. At ceiling level, any of the moldings shown in Figure 1-3(a) may be used, as well as a large variety of special ceiling moldings stocked at most building-supply houses.

6-4. How to Fur a Wall

When you wish to cover an existing wall with some sort of finished sheeting (such as finished plywood or decorative hardboard, for example), the wall must be flat. If the wall is irregular, such as a stone wall or broken plaster wall, some sort of flat surface must be added to the wall before applying the finishing. The usual method is to fur the wall. Furring material consists of flat boards 1″ thick and at least 2″ wide. These are nailed flat to the wall at convenient intervals, usually about 16″ apart. They are mounted horizontally and are nailed directly to the studs. Large, finished wallboards can then be nailed to the furring.

nailed to the side studs first. Then double thicknesses of 2″ × 3″ are nailed above and below. For wide windows, add the supporting vertical braces between the horizontal members and the plates.

If you are building a basement playroom or other area where two new walls are to meet at right angles, you will need a corner post. Make your own post by nailing three 2″ × 3″ together (Figure 6-5). Each 2″ × 3″ is cut to extend from floor to ceiling plates, and the post is toenailed to the plates.

Before covering the wall, install wiring and plumbing as required. This is one reason why these must be considered in the original plans. It is easier to install them before the wall is covered than to have to cut openings in the finished wall.

Gypsum wallboard and hardboard are the two favorites for covering the wall, although any of the materials listed in Table 6-1 can be used, as well as newer materials that are constantly being developed. When you select a wall material from the many available, make sure you buy the recommended nails to fasten the sheets to the studs. You will also need something to cover joints between sheets and nailheads. For some materials, a joint cement must be spread into the joint with a putty knife. The same cement is used to cover nailheads. For others, decorative adhesive strips are fastened over joints and nailheads.

For decorative purposes, you may want to conceal the joints where the wall meets the

If there are irregularities in the wall, the furring strips can be gouged out with a chisel to go over a projection or can be shimmed with wood scraps to go over a hollow. Use a level or plumb line to check that the furring is flat. Furring can be nailed directly to concrete walls using nails specially for this purpose.

Furring can also be used for new ceilings. When a ceiling is badly damaged, instead of trying to fix it, nail furring strips across the joists, right over the old ceiling. Then fasten wallboard to the furring.

6-5. How to Tile a Wall

Wall tiles are available in vinyl, plastic, metal, ceramic, etc. — in all the materials used for floor tiles. Whereas floor tiles are usually 9″ × 9″, most wall tiles are 4-1/2″ × 4-1/2″. Aside from this, the application methods are essentially the same.

As with floor tiles, you will need a few special tools for wall tiles. These include a spreader for the mastic and something to cut the tile. Plastic tiles can be cut with a small finishing saw or smooth hacksaw. Metal tiles can be cut with tin snips or a hacksaw. Ceramic tiles can be cut to fit by nibbling bits out with ordinary slip-joint pliers. When you buy tiles, you can also buy an inexpensive kit of tools to use specifically with the kind of tile you will use.

If you are tiling from some point above the floor, draw a line on all walls at the lowest level. Start tiling from this line. Use a level to make sure the line is horizontal. Do not trust your eyes for this.

Patch the wall before laying the tiles. Make sure the wall is smooth and clean. When laying a tile, try to place it down where it belongs. Do not slide it to its position. Most tiles require mastic, but some plastic wall tiles come with adhesive backing which will stick to plaster, wood and most wallboards.

You can use ceramic floor tiles to make a mosaic wall. Apply them to the wall in the same manner described in Section 5-7 for laying them on the floor. Ceramic tiles require grouting after they are laid. A ceramic wall requires almost no maintenance and is very easy to keep clean.

When a tile must be cut to fit into a space next to the wall, measure it in exactly the same manner as described for floor tiles. This is illustrated in Figure 5-8.

If a fixture is already fastened to the wall and cannot be moved, you can tile around it. If possible, however, try to attach fixtures later. Leave a space for the fixture, and fasten it to the wall so that its flange overlaps the tiles all around the space. In this way you avoid having to cut a tile. Alternatively, you can tile the whole wall and use fixtures that are fastened to the tiles by strong adhesives.

6-6. How to Repair a Tiled Wall

When one or more tiles in a wall are cracked, they are usually ignored. However, if the wall

is in the bathroom, water vapor can enter the cracks and cause damage to the wall under the tiles. The broken tiles should be removed and replaced with new ones. To remove the old tile, first scrape away the grout around it. You can use a beer can opener or a cold chisel to loosen the grout. Pry out the cracked tile or tiles with an old chisel or screwdriver, but be careful not to mar any of the adjacent tiles. Do not worry if the cracked tiles break up further.

After the old tile is removed, replace it with a new one as you would on a bare wall. Make sure that the wall underneath is clean. Add mastic and press in the new tile. Then apply grout around the tile.

When an opening appears around the tub in the bathroom at the junction of the wall, it is usually caused by settling. If the opening is small, clean out the old grout with any handy tool and recaulk the opening. Special silicone grouting is available in tubes and is very simple to apply. If the opening is too large for grouting, it can usually be covered with edging tiles made of ceramic or other materials to match your walls. These are tiles designed to attach to the tub and the wall and cover the back.

6-7. How to Install Shelves

Although a shelf can simply be nailed to a vertical member, this is undesirable, because the nails must support the entire weight on the shelf. The joint should be reinforced. Some methods of doing this are shown in Figure 6-6. In Figure 6-6(a), spacers are used between shelves to absorb and support the weight. This method makes very strong shelves. In Figure 6-6(b), cleats are used. These are nailed to the uprights, and the shelves are nailed to them.

For decorative purposes, the cleats can be quarter-round moldings or any other shape instead of rectangular. The channel, shown in Figure 6-6(c), is simple to install and useful in that shelves can be removed easily when desirable. The channel is usually made from

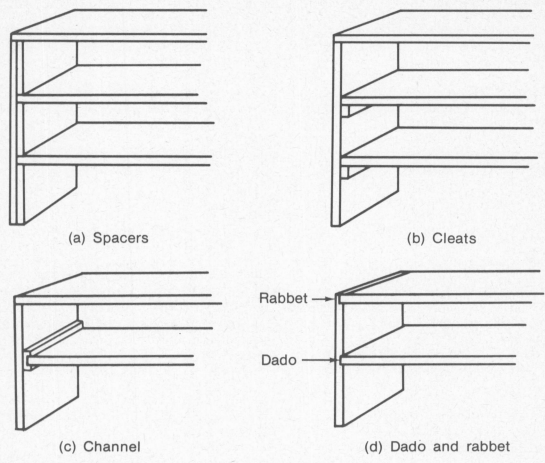

(a) Spacers

(b) Cleats

(c) Channel

(d) Dado and rabbet

Rabbet →

Dado →

Fig. 6-6. Shelving supports.

aluminum, although channels are available in brass, galvanized iron and other metals.

For a neat, professional-looking job, you may want to use one or more of the joints discussed in Section 1-3. Two of these are shown in Figure 6-6(d). The rabbet is used for the top shelf, and dadoes for lower shelves. Dowelling and other joints can also be used.

6-8. Wallpaper

Walls made of plaster or wallboard need some sort of finish to make them presentable. The simplest finish is paint, but wallpaper is economical and more decorative. Wallpaper comes in a great variety of colors, designs and materials. In addition to paper, wall materials include vinyl, canvas and other fabrics. All are usually referred to as *wallpaper* or *wall coverings*. Most of the wall materials, including paper, are water-resistant so that there is little danger of tearing wet paper when hanging them. And because they resist moisture, they are easily washed and can even be scrubbed. Many patterns and materials are available with adhesive backing, so that the messy job of mixing and applying paste is eliminated.

When you choose a wallpaper, you will be influenced by price. However, the first problem is to select a pattern that is acceptable. A common mistake is to choose a paper with a "cute" pattern that becomes boring after seeing it every day. Since it is much easier to work with prepasted paper, try to select a pattern in the prepasted materials carried by your dealer. Price is affected by quality, but it is also influenced by the design. Stripes, flowers, scenery and other simple patterns are usually less expensive than designs which simulate wood, velvet, or other materials.

The easiest way to find out how much paper to buy is to measure the room and then take the dimensions to your wallpaper dealer, and let him do the estimating. Remember to measure doors, windows and other openings that won't be covered, and subtract these areas from the overall area of the walls. The dealer will usually allow you to return un-started rolls, so it is a good idea to buy one or two extra in case you make a mistake.

Before hanging paper, make sure that the wall is sound. Patch all holes and cracks. If the wall has a coat of smooth paint or enamel on it, rub it with sandpaper to roughen it slightly. The wall should feel smooth, but paper will not cling as well to surfaces which are too smooth. Although it is preferable to remove the old paper, new wallpaper can be hung right over old wallpaper if the old surface is not torn or peeling. In this case, try to have the seams between sheets come between old seams, since if seams are lined up on top of each other, they become noticeable.

6-9. How to Remove Old Wallpaper

If the old wallpaper is torn, blistered or peeling, it should be removed before applying new paper. It is possible to scrape off old paper, but the quickest and best way is to steam it off with a wallpaper steamer. You can rent a steamer from your wallpaper dealer and finish the job in a fraction of the time it would take to scrape off the old paper. The rental cost is quite small compared to the cost of the wallpaper, so that it adds only a small percentage to the overall cost of the job.

A steaming machine has a boiler in which

water is heated by electricity in small units or by kerosene in larger ones. The steam from the boiling water is fed through a hose to a perforated plate which is held against the old wallpaper. The steam soaks into the paper, softening the paper and the paste holding it to the wall. The paper can then be stripped off the wall with a putty knife or any flat tool. A special tool for the purpose, called a *wall scraper*, looks like a very wide putty knife.

When using the machine, begin at the bottom of a wall, since the hot steam which rises will soften the paper above the plate as well as directly under it. Move the plate upward slowly with one hand while you strip the paper below with the other. Make sure the room is well ventilated to prevent it from filling up with steam.

The steamer can also be used to remove wallpaper from a papered ceiling. However, if paper is to be removed only from walls and it is desired to leave the old paper on a ceiling, you cannot use a steamer. The rising steam would loosen the ceiling paper. In this case, you will have to soak the paper on the wall by hand, preferably applying hot water with a large paintbrush or mop. You can also use a paint roller. When the paper is soaked, you will be able to strip it off with a flat tool.

Canvas-backed wallpaper is the easiest to remove; plastic-coated papers are the most difficult. In order to make the steam penetrate the plastic, it may be necessary to rub down the wall with coarse sandpaper. This scratches the plastic coating and lets the steam reach the paper below.

When you are finished removing the old paper, wipe up all excess moisture as soon as possible. Patch the wall where necessary to make a smooth surface for the new paper.

6-10. How to Hang Wallpaper

Before you begin, make sure you have the necessary tools. You will need a smoothing brush, a seam roller, sponge and a sharp razor blade mounted in a handle. You can buy a wallpaper tool kit which includes these tools as well as a wall scraper for removing old paper. These kits are inexpensive. A seam roller looks like a caster from a living room chair, and, in fact, if you don't have a seam roller you can use a caster instead. If you use prepasted paper, you will not have to mix paste and apply it. If not, you will need a paste brush and paste bucket in addition to the other tools.

The first step is to cut the paper into strips reaching from floor to ceiling, taking into consideration the necessity of fitting the pattern from one strip to the adjacent one. Allow 2″ or 3″ extra at each end of the strip. This excess will be cut off later. You should buy pretrimmed paper, which has the edges trimmed and is all ready for hanging. Pile up the strips, pattern side down, with the strip first to be hung on top of the pile and the strips arranged in the order in which they will be hung.

If you are using prepasted paper, this next step is eliminated, but if not, now is the time to apply paste. Paste is applied to one strip, and that strip is hung. Then paste is applied to the next, and so on. When using prepasted strips, follow the manufacturer's directions. The strips are usually soaked in a bathtub full of water or, if you want to be fancy, in a special wallpaper tank. One roll is soaked at a time. To apply paste to the unpasted paper, a long table is needed. A 5′ length of plywood on a bridge table makes a good temporary table. Place the strip on the table with the bottom end hanging off the end of the table. Apply paste with the brush to the part of the strip on the table. (Follow the manufacturer's directions for mixing the paste.) Now fold the bottom of the strip over toward the center, without creasing the paper, so that pasted surface is against pasted surface. Slide the

paper along the table so that the rest of the paper can now be pasted. You can now place the paper on the wall with its top at the ceiling. The bottom will be tucked under, making it easier to move the strip.

Begin next to a doorway. As you proceed around a room, the last strip will not have its pattern exactly matched to that of the first strip, but if the discontinuity is behind you as you enter the room, it is less noticeable. If there are large windows in the room, you can begin at a window edge, since the window becomes a break in the pattern.

Hang the first strip by placing the top half against the wall with its top edge 2″ or 3″ above the junction of wall and ceiling. Use a plumb line or vertical chalk line for the first strip. When the paper is properly lined up with the chalk line, smooth the upper half to the wall with the smoothing brush. Now pull down the portion that is tucked under, and smooth this to the wall, also. When all the bubbles are removed by smoothing, cut off the excess at top and bottom with your razor.

If the first strip is to go around a corner, have only about 1″ of width on one wall and the rest on the next wall. Line up the edge that is farther away from the corner with a plumb line. Walls do not always remain perpendicular to the floor and to each other, and it is possible that the 1″ width on the other wall will not be plumb to the floor. Every time you go around a corner, follow the same procedure of lining up the far edge with a true vertical.

After each strip is hung, sponge off the surface, being careful to remove all traces of paste. Also remove paste from floor and ceiling. After every two or three strips are hung, run the seam roller along the seams to press them firmly to the wall. With some papers, the manufacturer advises *not* using a seam roller. With these you can press seams to the wall with a damp sponge.

Plumbing

The usual plumbing system consists of two main subsystems, one to bring clean water into the house and the other to remove wastes. The water supply subsystem consists of a pipe which brings water into the house and branch pipes running to the water heater, to the faucets, and to other fixtures throughout the house. Water is fed to these fixtures by pressure in the city water pipes. The drain subsystem consists of drains in each sink, tub, and toilet which merge into a single, large drain pipe connected to a sewer, septic tank or cesspool. This subsystem works by gravity.

Although some plumbing jobs are too intricate or too distasteful for the average home owner, most of the problems can be solved easily by even an inexperienced handyman. You can fix leaks, noisy plumbing, frozen pipes, faulty fixtures and clogged drains, as well as adding a new faucet or replacing a fixture. A few minutes of your time and a small outlay for parts will frequently save you many dollars in plumber's bills.

7-1. How to Shut Off the Water Supply

The first thing you need to know about your plumbing is how to shut off the water. The main valve is usually near the water meter.

When a pipe develops a leak, the first thing that must be done is to shut off the main water supply.

This may be in the basement or utility room in temperate or frigid climates but may be outside the house in areas which never get frost. Turning the valve clockwise shuts off the water. To turn it back on again rotate the handle all the way anticlockwise. There are usually additional valves in the line to each fixture so that it is possible to shut off the water to a single faucet or toilet tank without shutting off all the water in the house. When a pipe breaks or a leak develops, the first thing to do is shut off the water and then decide what to do next. If in doubt as to which valve to shut off, always choose the main valve. Also, when you are about to make any repair in the water line, shut off the water to the fixture you will work on either in the line to the fixture or at the main valve. Don't forget to turn on the water when you finish the repair.

7-2. Frozen Pipes

If you take the precautions mentioned in Volume 1 you should never have to worry about a frozen pipe. Nevertheless, sometimes a sudden cold spell during the night can catch you by surprise and freeze the water in a pipe leading to the outside of the house. The danger is that you will not notice it, since you will not be using the outside faucet, and then the expanding ice will rupture the pipe. If there is a frost and you have forgotten to shut off the water to outside faucets, do so at the first opportunity. After closing the valve in the pipe leading to the outside tap, open the tap and allow the water in the pipe to flow out. If no water comes out, the pipe may already be frozen.

Frozen pipes can also occur when a pipe inside the house is too close to an open window or passes through an unheated part of the basement or attic. You will be aware that something is wrong when you open a faucet, and the water trickles out too slowly or doesn't flow at all. Similarly, a hot-water radiator near an open window can freeze if the outside temperature is far below freezing. Prevention is easy. Don't open windows near radiators or pipes and keep basements warmed at least slightly in any part containing water pipes.

If you do find a frozen pipe or radiator, you must take steps immediately to thaw it before the expanding ice causes a rupture. In the case of a radiator, close the outside window and simply apply heat to the radiator. You can use hot towels, a heating pad, an electric hair dryer, a soldering iron or any source of heat you have available. If the room is warm, you can just let nature take its course; the ice will melt eventually, although more slowly than if direct heat is applied.

If a water pipe is frozen, find the location of the ice by running your hand along the pipe to the coldest spot. First, open the faucet. Then apply heat to the frozen pipe. You can use a small propane torch, if you have one, being careful not to burn the walls or ceiling. If you have a soldering iron, you can strap it to the pipe with the hot tip in contact with the pipe. Heat from the iron will be conducted along the pipe in both directions.

WARNING: When you use a torch or soldering iron, you may generate enough heat to boil the water inside the pipe. The steam must have some means of escape, or it can burst the pipe. Consequently, use these heating devices *only on the faucet side* of the ice block. Then the steam can come out of the open faucet. This is not a danger if you use a milder source of heat such as hot towels or a hair dryer. When the ice has melted, indicated by a flow of water from the faucet, close the faucet and inspect the pipe for leaks. If there is a leak, repair it as described in the next section. If the temperature is not too low or if you act quickly enough, the ice will not have expanded enough to cause damage. Don't consider the job complete until you have taken steps to prevent a recurrence of the trouble.

7-3. Leaks in Water Pipes

Leaks can occur in water pipes where the pipe is screwed into a threaded joint. There is no

Pipe-sealing compound is one of various ways to repair a leak to a threaded joint.

actual break in the pipe, but the sealing compound in the joint may have dried out. Leaks also occur if the pipe is broken or cracked, such as might happen from expanding ice in the pipes. In any case, you must correct the defect quickly to prevent water damage.

If the leak is easily apparent, you will know whether water is leaking from a joint or from a hole in the pipe. If the pipe is inside a wall and your first sign of trouble is water leaking on the floor or a damp wall, you will have to rip open a partition in the wall to determine the source of the leak. Don't be afraid to do this, since a plumber would have to do it anyway before he could fix the pipe. Inspect both sides of the wall to determine which can be opened with a minimum of damage. In any case, whether the leak is in the open or hidden in the wall, your first step is to turn off the water in the pipe.

If the leak is at a threaded joint, you can sometimes stop it simply by screwing the pipe farther into the joint. To do this, you will need two wrenches, one to hold the joint and the other to turn the pipe. If you use only one wrench on the pipe itself, you may twist the joint and cause a break in the pipe on the other side.

NOTE: When you screw the pipe into the joint, you will be unscrewing it from a joint at the other end. Nevertheless, sometimes a quarter- or half-turn may be enough to stop the leak without causing trouble at the other end.

You can also seal the joint with an epoxy patching material, available in most hardware stores. Full directions for mixing and applying the chemicals are given on the package. The most important step is to make certain that the surface of the pipe is *clean* and *dry* before applying the patching compound. The same epoxy compound can also be used to seal small holes and cracks in pipes. The compound should be allowed to harden for about twelve hours before the water is turned on again.

Ordinary pipe-sealing compound can also be used to cure a leaking joint. Unscrew the pipe, coat the threads with the compound, and then screw the pipe back into the joint.

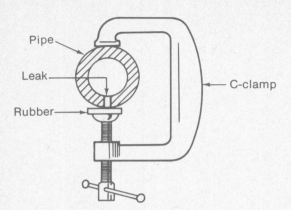

Fig. 7-1. Temporary repair for leak.

again on top of the fiberglas. This type of patch is permanent and should outlast the pipe. Again, the most important step in putting on the patch is to make sure that the pipe is clean and dry.

Unfortunately, leaks usually happen on weekends or at night when hardware stores are closed. If you have no patching material, you can make a temporary repair (Figure 7-1). A piece of rubber, such as a strip from an old inner tube, is held against the leak with a C-clamp. After the hardware store is open, you can buy a patching kit for a permanent repair. Stores also sell pipe clamps and plugs for sealing small leaks. These work on much the same principle as the C-clamp in Figure 7-1. The advantage of the clamp over the epoxy patching compound is that the pipe is usable immediately after putting on the clamp. The clamp is supposed to be a temporary repair, but some have been in use for years.

If the pipe is badly corroded or has a wide split, it should be replaced. Use a hacksaw to cut the pipe near the middle, and then unscrew each half from its joint, using two wrenches, one on the pipe and one to hold the joint. Measure the distance between the two joints. Take one of the pieces of pipe as a sample to a plumbing supply store and explain that you want that kind of pipe to cover the measured distance (you will need pipe somewhat longer to include the thread that goes into the joint). The replacement should consist of two pieces of pipe and a *union* that goes between them, as shown in Figure 7-2. Each of the two pieces of pipe is

Again, as you unscrew the pipe from one joint, you screw it into another at the other end of the pipe. To seal both joints, first unscrew the pipe at one joint and coat it with the compound. Then screw it back far enough to unscrew the other end and coat that end also. Finally, screw it back into the second joint so that it goes approximately the same distance into each joint. If you want to reinforce the joint, you can wrap fine cotton thread or string around the threads on the pipe after you coat it with the pipe compound. The string swells when wet and acts as an additional seal, although in most cases the sealing compound alone is sufficient.

If the leak is in the pipe itself, it can be fixed with epoxy compound, as described above. For larger leaks and cracks, patching kits are available, consisting of fiberglas cloth, which is wrapped around the pipe, and epoxy compound, which is applied first and then

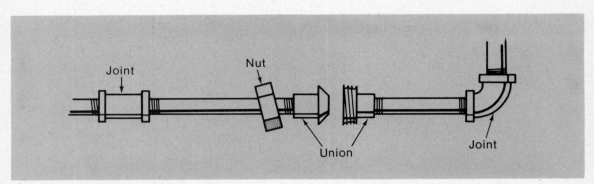

Fig. 7-2. Pipe replacement with union.

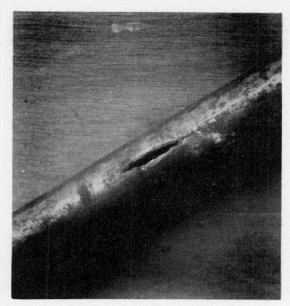

To repair a cracked pipe, buy a patching kit containing fiberglas cloth and epoxy compound.

threaded at both ends. One pipe is threaded into each joint, and half of the union is threaded on each pipe. Make certain that you slip on the coupling nut before you screw on the union. The union permits joining the pipes without twisting them. The two halves of the union are held together by tightening the coupling nut with an adjustable wrench. A packing gasket inside the nut prevents a leak at the union. Threading pipe is simple if you have the proper tools, but since you are unlikely to have them, buy pipe already threaded.

7-4. Dripping Faucets

Part of a conventional faucet is shown in Figure 7-3. The valve stem screws into the body of the faucet. The stem washer, which is held at the bottom of the stem by a brass screw, fits into a valve seat when the stem is all the way down, and thus closes off the opening for the flow of water. When the handle is turned, the coarse thread on the stem lifts the stem and washer off the valve seat,

permitting water to flow. The bonnet screws onto the main body of the faucet and prevents you from turning the handle so far that the valve stem comes clear of the faucet body. Packing in the bonnet prevents water from leaking up between the stem and bonnet.

Each time the faucet is closed, the washer is compressed against the valve seat and at the same time rotated against it. This constant rubbing slowly wears away the washer so that eventually it no longer fits tightly against the valve seat. Then the faucet will drip even when the stem is apparently all the way down. This may not be annoying but it is a waste of water that can be expensive. Furthermore, it can only get worse.

When a closed faucet drips, you can usually fix it simply by replacing the washer. First, shut off the water running to the faucet; then remove the handle. The handle is held onto the stem by a screw, but the screw may be covered with a decorative plate. The plate may be held on by a knurled collar, which must be twisted off, or by friction, in which case it can be pried off with a small screwdriver. At any rate, unscrew the screw holding the handle and lift off the handle. Then unscrew the bonnet from the body of the faucet, using an adjustable wrench, and slide it off the stem. Now you can unscrew the stem completely from the faucet. You may find it easier to put the handle back on the stem to rotate it out of the faucet. You can now get at the washer on the end of the stem.

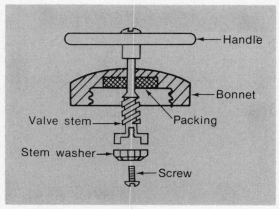

Fig. 7-3. Parts of faucet.

When a closed faucet drips, you can usually fix it by replacing the washer.

better to find the size you need and buy some of that size only. Replace the screw holding the new washer, again being careful not to gouge your hand with the screwdriver. Before putting the stem back into the faucet, look at the valve seat and feel it with your finger. It should be smooth. If it has rough edges or if there is grit on it, the new washer will soon be chewed up. You can buy a very inexpensive seat-dressing tool to smooth a rough valve seat. Let the hardware dealer show you how to work it. It will save replacing a lot of washers.

If the faucet leaks at the top of the bonnet either when it is open or shut, the packing in the bonnet is worn. With the faucet apart, dig out the old packing from the bonnet with a screwdriver and install new packing. Packing material looks like heavy string impregnated with graphite. Wind it around the stem until it fills the bonnet cavity. It is usually held in place with a packing nut. Some faucets use a plastic ring as the packing material, and plastic rings may be available as a replacement for the old packing on older faucets. If you need new packing, take the bonnet with you when you visit the hardware dealer and let him tell you what to use. Don't forget to turn on the water again after the faucet is repaired.

WARNING: Many people have gouged their hands with screwdrivers while trying to remove the screw at the end of the stem. If you hold the stem in one hand and apply a screwdriver with the other, there is a tendency to push the hands toward each other as you turn the screw. If for any reason the screwdriver slips, it moves very rapidly toward the hand holding the valve stem. To prevent this, do not use pressure as you turn this screw. Better still, put the stem in a vise instead of holding it in your hand.

After you remove the washer, replace it with a new one of the same size. You can buy an assortment of washers of different sizes very inexpensively, but most of them won't fit. It's

7-5. How to Add a Faucet

If you need an extra faucet, for a washing machine for example, it is very simple to add a *saddle type* of faucet to an existing iron or copper pipe. This type of faucet is available in a kit, containing all needed parts and complete instructions. It is not necessary to disconnect any pipes to install the new faucet. First make sure that the pipe is smooth and clean. Then strap the saddle faucet to the pipe (Figure 7-4). The two bolts in the bracket are tightened until the faucet is firmly in place. The point of contact between the faucet and the pipe is a rubber washer, which prevents leaks. After the faucet is in place, shut off the water in the pipe. Then remove the bonnet and the valve stem. Insert a drilling guide that

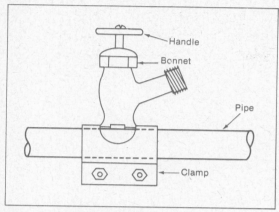

Fig. 7-4. Saddle-type faucet.

comes with the kit and run a 1/4-inch drill through the wall of the pipe, being careful not to drill into the other side. Remove the drilling guide and blow out the chips of metal, but protect your eyes as you do so. Put back the stem and screw on the bonnet, and the job is complete. Turn the water on again, and open the new faucet to flush out any metal chips remaining in the pipe. This type of faucet may be mounted in any convenient position on either a horizontal or vertical pipe.

7-6. Types of Pipe

The pipe shown in Figure 7-2 is usually made of iron or steel and is joined with threaded fittings or joints. Although it is easily cut with a hacksaw, the home owner rarely has occasion to do anything to this type of pipe except screw in new sections or seal holes, as indicated in Section 7-3. If new pipe is needed, it can be bought cut to length and already threaded. Fittings are available in a variety of shapes, including elbows, tees, 45° bends and others.

If it is necessary to add a water pipe to your plumbing to bring water to a new fixture, for example, it is not difficult to replace an existing elbow or joint with a tee and screw the new pipe in the third arm of the tee. Any

new pipe must be properly supported by brackets so that there is no strain at the joints.

Copper pipe or tubing is frequently used for new water lines because it is easy to handle, can be bent around obstacles, and requires only a few tools for installation. The tubing is cut to length with a fine-toothed hacksaw or an inexpensive tubing cutter. It is soldered to fittings with a propane torch. If you are going to add extensive plumbing to your home, you should use copper tubing rather than iron water pipes. Although copper is more expensive, it will outlast iron. Also, if water in copper tubing freezes, it is not as likely to rupture the pipe, since copper is a softer metal and can be stretched slightly without damage.

Soldering copper pipe is relatively simple, even if you've never soldered anything before. A typical connection of three pipes in a tee is shown in Figure 7-5. The ends of the pieces of tubing are polished with steel wool before inserting them in the junction. (In the figure, a tee is shown, but there are a variety of other fittings or junctions, including an adaptor to connect copper tubing to existing iron pipe.) The inside of the junction should also be cleaned with steel wool. After the parts are cleaned, the polished end of each piece of tubing is coated with soldering paste, and the pipes are then inserted in the junction. Heat is applied to the fitting by directing the flame from your propane torch to the fitting itself and not to the copper pipes. As the fitting gets hot, heat is conducted to the pipes, and they soon get hot enough to melt the solder. The flame is never directed at the solder or the

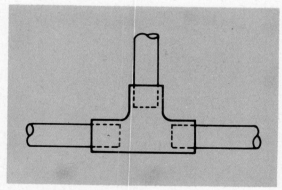

Fig. 7-5. Junction in copper tubing.

Types of pipe and joints.

tubing but is kept on the junction during the whole operation. The solder comes in a roll and looks like stiff wire. A convenient length, perhaps 6 or 8 inches, is unrolled from the reel, and with the reel in the hand that is not holding the torch, the end of the solder is applied at the points where the tubing enters the fitting. As the solder melts, it is drawn into the junction by capillary action. Each solder joint should use about 1″ of the wire solder. As soon as enough solder has been sucked in to surround the pipe completely, remove the torch and wipe away any excess solder on the outside of the joint with a heavy cloth while the solder is still molten.

The cost of a propane torch is not justified if you need to make only one or two connections, but for an extensive installation the price of the torch is a very small part of the total outlay and can be considered part of the materials bill. Even though you may never

have another plumbing job, you will find other uses for the torch, such as removing paint, defrosting pipes, heating metal for bending, starting charcoal fires, and as a cookstove when camping.

The drainage system in a home is made up of pipes and traps from each fixture, which empty into a large pipe. This pipe carries the waste to the sewer or septic tank. The pipes from the sinks and the traps are usually made of chrome-plated brass. Sections are coupled with large nuts which can be loosened or tightened with a large adjustable wrench or a Stillson wrench. If you use a Stillson wrench, you should protect the chrome surfaces from the serrated jaws by padding the jaws with a few layers of cloth. The pipes themselves do not rotate; only the nuts need be turned to disassemble or assemble these pipes. The large pipe which receives the waste from sinks, tubs, showers and other similar fixtures is called a *waste pipe*. The pipe that receives discharge from toilets is called a *soil pipe*. Both are usually made of cast iron and require special fittings. Repairing cast-iron pipe is a job for a professional plumber.

A recent development is plastic pipe, available in many different sizes, for use both for water pipes and for drains, including replacement for the large cast-iron pipes.

Plastic pipe is so simple to use with a minimum of tools that home owners can do all their own plumbing jobs wherever it is permitted. The pipe is flexible so that it can be bent around obstructions. It is light enough for one person to handle. As a contrast, cast-iron soil pipe weighs about 10 pounds per foot, whereas the equivalent plastic pipe weighs less than 1-1/2 pounds per foot.

Plastic pipe cannot yet be used for hot-water lines, because the material may deteriorate at hot-water temperatures. Improved plastics for hot-water use are being developed, and eventually plastic will be available for all plumbing.

Sections of plastic pipe are easily joined by slipping the end of each pipe over a serrated coupling section and tightening the connection with an ordinary hose clamp. Only a screwdriver is needed to make the connection. Special tees, elbows and other fittings are available, and the pipe can be attached to them in the same manner or cemented in place. Adaptors are also available for attaching plastic pipe to metal pipe. To cut plastic pipe, you need only a hacksaw. If the edges are burred, you can smooth them with sandpaper, a file or even a paring knife. If you wish to cement the pipe to a fitting, an applicator comes with the special cement; so you don't need any other tools.

One big advantage of plastic pipe is that it is not damaged by freezing. It simply expands with the ice. Thus it can be used for a sprinkler system for your lawn, buried only a few inches below the surface. When it freezes in winter, you can ignore it. In the spring after it thaws, it will be as good as new.

There are many different plastic materials used for pipe, and each has its own advantages and disadvantages. A few are listed here:

Polyethylene is the cheapest and is available in rolls up to 400' long. It is most useful for bringing water into the house. A single length can be run from the water meter to the house inlet; it will require then only two fittings, one at each end.

Poly(vinyl chloride) (PVC) is slightly more expensive and is ideally suited for sprinkler systems and for carrying drinking water. It is available in rigid lengths of up to 10'.

Acrylonitrite butadiene styrene (ABS) is a lightweight, almost frictionless pipe especially adapted for waste removal to replace the common cast-iron waste or soil pipe. It is available in 10' lengths, with diameters ranging from about 1-1/2" to 4".

Styrene pipe has thin walls and is available in 10' lengths of 3" or 4" diameter for special drainage applications.

If plastic pipe is permitted by your building code, you can plan on using it for new or replacement applications in your home. For most cold-water pipes in the home, choose PVC. Let your hardware dealer show you the many connectors and adaptors for use with this plastic. You can even use small lengths of PVC to replace sections of broken steel or copper pipe. For large waste drains you can install ABS tubing yourself. If it is a replacement for a damaged soil pipe, the hardest part of the job will be the removal of the heavy cast-iron pipe. New installations must be approved by your local plumbing inspector, so you should submit plans to him before you start work. Dealers who sell ABS pipe can supply you with the necessary information as well as directions for installing ABS drains, pipes and vents.

7-7. Noisy Plumbing

Plumbing is supposed to be relatively quiet. If your plumbing system bangs or hammers when you shut off a faucet or chatters or whistles when you turn one on, it is not in normal condition and should be corrected. Although such noises do not signal a dangerous situation, they are annoying and should be eliminated, since the situation causing the noise can only get worse.

Chattering or whistling that occurs when a faucet is first opened or just before the last turn of closing may be caused by a worn washer in the faucet, worn packing or a damaged valve seat. Check the washer first. If it is loose, tighten the screw holding it. If it is worn, replace it. If the washer is not at fault and the valve seat seems all right, replace the packing. You can check the valve seat by running your finger over it. It should feel smooth to the touch with no burrs or metal chips in it.

A banging or hammering sound in the pipes *when a faucet is closed quickly* is called *water hammer.* It is caused by the sudden stopping of the flow of water. Since water is incompressible, the energy of its forward motion bangs back and forth in the pipe until the vibrations die down. Sometimes this noise is accentuated by loosely mounted pipe which is set in motion by the water vibrations and then bangs against the beams. As a first step, make sure that each pipe is rigidly mounted. Tighten supporting braces along its length and at corners. Iron water pipe should be supported by braces no more than 6′ apart. Copper pipes need somewhat less support. It is interesting to note that hammer rarely occurs in plastic pipe, since the plastic can expand and absorb the shock.

If all else fails, you should consider adding an air cushion to your system to absorb the energy of the stopped flow of water. Two configurations are shown in Figure 7-6. In each, a tee is placed in the line to the faucet and a sealed pipe is added to the third arm of the tee. The third arm contains air, but since the pipe is sealed, the air cannot escape. When the faucet is closed, the energy in the motion of water pushes some water into the air chamber, where the air compresses and absorbs the shock. The air chamber should be placed close to the noisy faucet to be most effective, but it will work anywhere in the water line.

In most new plumbing systems, air cushions are installed in the system when the house is first built. If your plumbing was quiet and has now developed a noise, an existing air

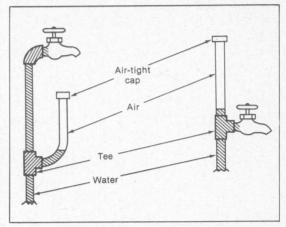

Fig. 7-6. Air cushion to eliminate water hammer.

cushion might be full of water because of a faulty seal at the end. If this happens, drain the water from the pipe and apply sealing compound to the cap on the end of the air pipe. In Figure 7-6, notice that the cushion can be below the faucet, as at the left, or above it, as at the right. If the air chamber is *above* the faucet, it is easily drained by opening the faucet after the water is shut off. To drain the air cushion at the left, it is necessary to open a faucet at a lower level. After the pipe is drained and resealed, the water can be turned on again. If all this sounds like too much work, you can prevent water hammer by shutting off faucets *slowly.*

Pounding, creaking and rumbling noises can occur in hot-water pipes when water is too hot. Water should never be hotter than 140° F. Noises in hot-water pipes may indicate that the temperature is too high and the hot-water heater should be checked. Creaking can also be caused by hot-water pipes expanding as hot water replaces cold inside the pipes. As they expand, they may rub against the beams. If you can locate the point of rubbing, you can eliminate the noise by inserting a piece of heat-resistant material, such as asbestos, between the pipe and the beam.

A humming noise when water is flowing in pipes is usually caused by the pipes being tightly fastened to the wooden structures of the house. The hum should normally be barely discernible, but when the pipes are in close contact with the beams, the wood acts like a sounding board to magnify the noise. To loosen the pipes would only cause other noises due to vibration, but the hum can be minimized by inserting bits of foam rubber, sponge or scraps of a soft material like felt where the pipe touches the wood.

7-8. Traps and Vents

The drainage system in your home empties directly into a sewer or septic tank. Drain pipes from sinks, showers and the like (*waste pipes*) and those from toilets (*soil pipes*) are positioned so that all waste flows to the sewer by gravity. An important consideration in the design of a plumbing system is provision for preventing sewer gases from entering the house through the same pipes that carry the waste to the sewer. Sewer gases have an offensive odor and, when under pressure, are explosive. What is needed is some sort of valve which will permit water and wastes to flow unhindered toward the sewer but which will not allow gases to flow from the sewer back into the house. There is such a device, and it is extremely simple. It is called a *trap*.

A trap is simply a U-shaped section of pipe which is filled with water in normal use, as in Figure 7-7. As water flows from the sink into

When removing a sink trap, protect the chromium fixture with tape or cloth.

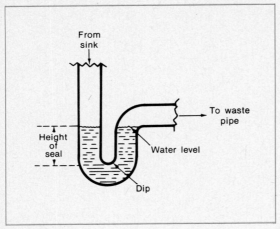

Fig. 7-7. Trap.

the trap, it raises the water level above the height of the output pipe. Thus, water flows out to the waste pipe as fast as water flows into the trap, but the trap remains full of water, as shown. Any gases coming from the waste pipe are prevented from entering by this *water seal* in the trap. The output pipe of the trap may extend horizontally through the wall to a waste pipe or may curve again and pass straight down to a waste pipe below the floor.

NOTE: As long as the water level in the trap is above the *dip* – that is, the bottom of the inside curve of the U – the trap is an effective seal, but if the water level sinks below this point, gases can pass through the trap.

A toilet also has a water seal or trap which operates on much the same principle (Figure 7-8). Again, as long as the water level is above the *dip,* gases are prevented from entering.

A trap is necessary in the drainage line from every sink, tub, shower or other water fixture. It is also needed in any drain that empties into a waste line, such as a drain in the floor of a garage or basement.

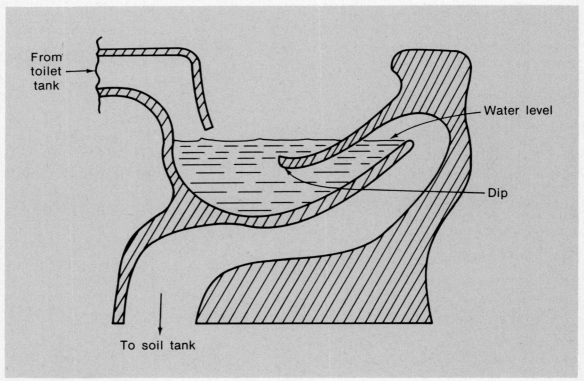

Fig. 7-8. Water seal in toilet.

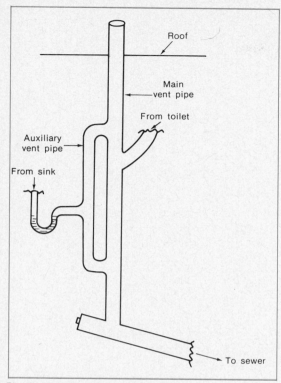

Fig. 7-9. Vented plumbing system.

Although the trap solves the problem of keeping sewer gases out of the house, any gas in the pipe between a trap and the sewer is a potential hazard because of the danger of explosion. To solve this, the drainage system must be *vented* so that the dangerous gases in the pipe can be exhausted harmlessly into the atmosphere. A vented plumbing system is shown in Figure 7-9. The main vent is usually a large cast-iron pipe extending from the soil pipe at the lowest level up through the roof of the house. The dangerous sewer gases are lighter than air, and, therefore, they pass right up this pipe into the atmosphere. They are prevented from entering the house through any drain line by traps in every line. A separate auxiliary vent pipe is used on each fixture, as shown in the figure. Otherwise, the seal in a lower-level trap might be broken by siphoning when a toilet is flushed at a higher level. This can be explained by imagining that the toilet and sink in Figure 7-9 both feed into the main vent pipe and that there is no

auxiliary pipe. Now, when the toilet is flushed, a large amount of water rushes down this main vent past the point where the sink trap joins the pipe. The rush of water creates a suction which draws the water out of the trap in the sink. Then the sink trap ceases to be a seal and remains in this condition until more water is poured into the drain in the sink. The auxiliary vent pipe prevents the siphoning created by the large flow of water from the flushed toilet.

Your own plumbing system should have been vented properly when installed. However, if you are going to install extra fixtures anywhere in the house, it is important to make sure that they are vented as required by your local plumbing code. The dealer who sells you the fixture can explain what venting is required and can be helpful in planning the layout. If the new fixture is on the ground floor, the drain should empty into a waste pipe or soil pipe. On an upper floor, the drain can be attached to the large vent pipe that goes through the roof. In either case, additional venting is required and can be achieved by tapping into an auxiliary vent pipe. This means that your new fixture should be near an existing vent pipe. If not, you will have to add a vent pipe, which means a combination of plumbing work, roofing work and carpentry. You will save yourself much work and money if you plan your new fixture close to a vent pipe. You can determine the location of vents simply by looking at your roof and seeing where they protrude.

7-9. Clogged Plumbing

All the drains in the house empty into a large waste pipe or soil pipe. The fixtures on upper floors are always close to a vertical stack pipe which runs from the large waste pipe at the lowest level up through the roof. The waste pipe is usually in the basement or under the house, and it slopes toward the sewer. When there is a stoppage in the drain system, your repair procedure will depend to a certain extent upon where the stoppage is located, and your first step is to determine the location of the fault.

If a single sink is blocked, and all other fixtures drain properly, the fault must be in the sink drain. On the other hand, if water emptying from one fixture backs up into another, the drains of both fixtures are probably all right, but the blockage must be located in a pipe into which both of these drains empty. On an upper floor of the house, because of the short runs between each fixture and the vertical stack, you will be able to locate the blockage easily. The vertical stack rarely gets clogged. If two fixtures on an upper floor empty into the same short drain to the vertical stack, and if water from one backs up in the other, the blockage is in that short length of pipe to the stack. On the first floor where fixtures empty directly into the waste pipe, a blockage in the waste pipe can affect all the drains that precede the blockage. You can determine the approximate location of the blockage by noticing which fixtures are clogged and which flow freely. The blockage in the waste pipe must be between the last fixture that is clogged and the first that is free.

Stoppages are caused by foreign matter in the drain. In bathroom sinks and tubs the most common cause of a blockage is hair in the drain. Lint and soap are also offenders. In kitchen sinks, cold grease is the most common cause of a stoppage, but food particles of all sorts are also frequent sources of trouble. In toilets, too large a wad of paper or other foreign matter can cause a blockage, as can soap, a comb, a toothbrush, or anything else dropped in accidentally.

Unless something large such as a dishrag or a comb is dropped into a drain, stoppages do not occur suddenly. You will notice first that water is not flowing out of a drain as fast as it should. This is a sign that a blockage is developing. When food or other matter partially blocks a drain, it slows the water running out, but also other particles of food or lint catch on the partial blockage and further restrict the flow of water, until eventually there is complete stoppage. It is easier to correct a partial blockage than a complete stoppage, so be alert to the possibility and take correc-

tive action when you first notice a drain emptying too slowly.

When you first notice a slowdown in the drain, check for lint or hair in the path of the water. In bathroom sinks that have a stopper actuated by a metal handle near the faucets, hair frequently catches on the stopper and obstructs the flow of water. Pull out the stopper and remove hair and other dirt from it. In most sinks the stopper can be removed by rotating it counterclockwise. Just cleaning the stopper will frequently cure the trouble. Hair on the stopper also may prevent the stopper from sealing the opening completely, so that water leaks out of the sink when the stopper should be closed. Removing the hair will cure this condition also.

If removing obvious hair or lint at the entrance to the drain does not cure the trouble, your next step should be to try to force the obstruction through the drain into the larger stack or waste pipe by using the old plumber's helper, the force cup or plunger. The cup of the plunger is placed over the drain opening (Figure 7-10). If the sink has an overflow pipe as shown in this figure, the opening of the overflow must be stopped up by stuffing a towel or face cloth into it. This will cause the force of the plunger to be directed into the drain instead of out the overflow. The water level in the sink should be at least one inch above the bottom of the plunger. If there is only a partial stoppage in the sink, fill the sink nearly full so that some water will remain while you use the plunger. Now press the plunger up and down several times. The down strokes will exert pressure on the blockage to force it toward the main drain. The up strokes will tend to pull any loose dirt out of the drain up into the sink. Don't give up too soon. It may take a dozen attempts before the plunger clears the drain.

For a partial blockage, you can also try a caustic drain cleaner. This is available in most supermarkets. *Before using it, read the instructions on the can.* These drain cleaners can be dangerous if used incorrectly.

WARNING: Despite manufacturer's recommendations, you should *not* use a caustic cleaner to try to clear a drain that is

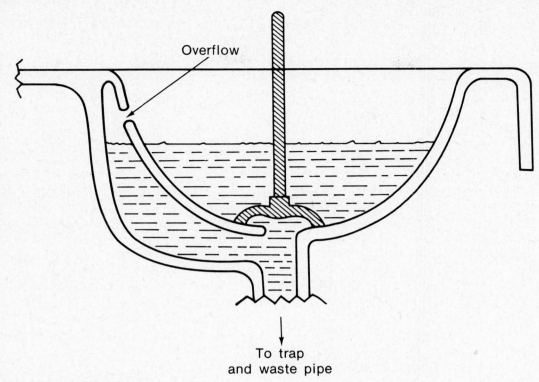

Overflow

To trap
and waste pipe

Fig. 7-10. How to use plunger.

completely blocked. These cleaners work on hair, soap or food particles, but if the drain is clogged from a dishrag, for example, the caustic cleaner may not work, and then you will have a pipe full of a dangerous chemical. For most partial blockages, these cleaners clear the debris. After using a caustic cleaner, run cold water through the cleared drain to clean out the chemical.

WARNING: Do *not* use a caustic cleaner in a kitchen sink equipped with a garbage disposer. The chemical can damage the disposer.

If the blockage cannot be cleared with a plunger or chemical, it will be necessary to use a special tool called a pipe *auger* or *plumber's snake.* The snake is a long flexible steel cable which can be inserted into a drain or other opening and can be made to pass through curved pipe to the obstruction. A handle on one end is rotated and causes the tip inside the pipe to rotate. Various tips are

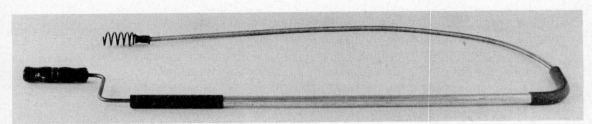

Plumber's snake.

used. A serrated tip will cut through a grease plug, breaking it into small particles which can be washed down the drain. A hook can be used to snare a dishrag and pull it out.

It is possible to insert the snake into the drain and push it into and through the trap until it hits the obstruction. It is easier, however, to remove the trap and insert the snake into the drain pipe leading into the wall or floor (Figure 7-11). To remove the trap, it is only necessary to unscrew two floating nuts, one on each side of the U-shaped trap, and then to pull gently on the U until it comes off. Since the trap is full of water and the drain to the sink above it is also full of water, you should put a pail or dishpan under the trap before you remove it. When you have removed the trap, check to see that it is clear, and if necessary, clean it. It may be that a trap blocked with grease is the cause of the stoppage. If the trap is clear, insert the snake in the pipe, as in Figure 7-11, and rotate the handle, pushing the snake into the pipe as you do so. When you feel the blockage, keep

rotating the handle. If the blockage is caused by food particles or grease, the tip of the snake will break it up. If the obstruction is a rag, the tip will snag it. Now you can pull out the snake with the rag attached. As you withdraw the snake, continue rotating it, in the same direction as you turned it when you inserted it. If you turn it in the opposite direction, it may be unhooked from the cloth you are trying to pull out. After clearing the drain, put back the trap, making sure that the washers inside the nuts are properly replaced.

If a drain leaks at one of the nuts, it is almost certainly a defective washer. Simply replace it. You will have to specify the size of pipe in the drain when buying a new washer, or take the nut along with you and get a washer that fits into it.

If a toilet is clogged from too much paper or a piece of cloth, the obstruction can frequently be pushed through with a plunger. Again, don't give up too soon. After the obstruction is apparently cleared, you should

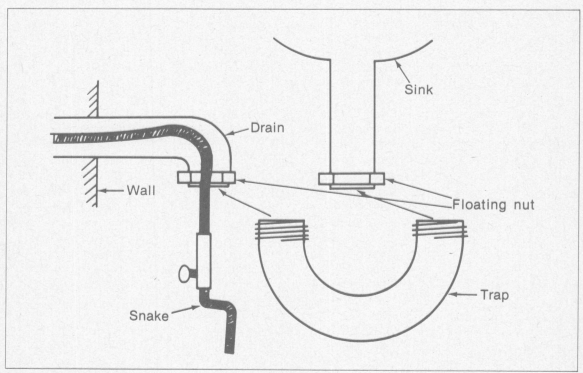

Fig. 7-11. How to use snake.

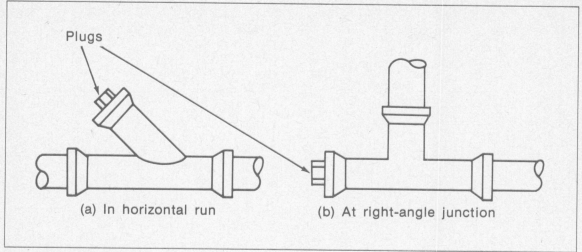

(a) In horizontal run   (b) At right-angle junction

Fig. 7-12. Clean-out plugs.

check the toilet by dropping a length of toilet paper about 5 feet long into it and flushing the toilet. If the paper goes through, the obstruction is cleared, but if it blocks again, the obstruction is probably a toothbrush or comb that was dropped in accidentally. You can try to pull it out with a hook on the end of a snake, but it is difficult. If you can't remove an object like a comb dropped in the toilet bowl, you will have to call a plumber. He will remove the bowl from the floor, empty it, and put it back in place. This job is too complicated for the home repairman.

If the obstruction is in a main drain, you can clear it with a snake. Every large waste pipe in the home should have a clean-out plug, as shown in Figure 7-12. The plug has a hexagonal head and can be removed with a Stillson wrench or an adjustable wrench. Slide the snake into the opening and along the pipe until you hit the obstruction, then operate as described above. When the pipe is clear, flush it with clean water to wash all particles of dirt out of the system. If the flow of water is slow but not stopped, you can add a chemical cleaner. Heed the precautions on the can.

For most jobs a 15' snake will clear the obstruction. Longer snakes up to 50' are available, as well as electrically operated ones. These can be rented if needed. They will be used rarely.

7-10. Toilet Tanks

There are two separate mechanisms in a flush tank, one for emptying the water and the second for filling. When the handle on the tank is turned, water rushes out of the tank into the toilet by gravity, causing the toilet to be flushed. As soon as the water starts to run out of the tank, the filling mechanism starts to operate, but the water is rushing out faster than the water coming in. When the tank is nearly empty, the opening to the outlet closes, and the tank soon fills. The valve controlling the incoming water closes when the tank is filled.

The mechanism to empty the tank and flush the toilet is shown in Figure 7-13. The water level in the tank is normally about 1 inch below the top of the overflow tube. When the handle is turned to flush the toilet, the right end of the *trip lever* is raised and pulls on the *linkage wire*. This in turn catches the loop at the top of the *lift rod* and thus raises the *flush ball,* which closes the opening to the toilet. With the flush ball raised, water rushes through the opening into the toilet. The buoyancy of the flush ball keeps it raised as long as there is water above the level of the opening. When most of the water has left the

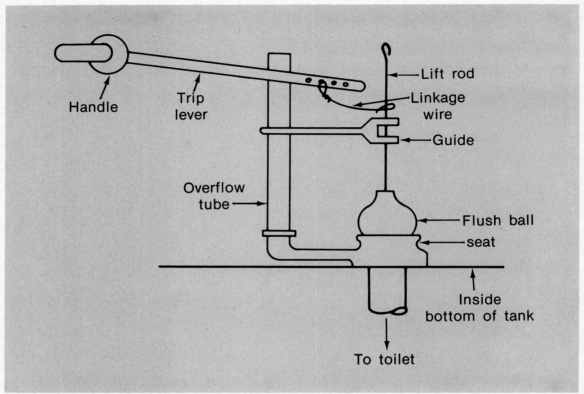

Fig. 7-13. Flushing mechanism.

tank, the flush ball falls back into the *seat,* closing the opening to the toilet pipe. The pressure of the water in the tank holds the ball on the seat despite its buoyancy, but once the ball is lifted it stays up as long as there is water to hold it. If the water does not shut off when the tank is refilled the water level will rise to the top of the overflow tube and any excess will flow down this tube, under the flush ball, and into the toilet.

The mechanism for refilling the tank is shown in Figure 7-14. The water entering from the pipe below the tank is stopped by a washer on a *plunger* that blocks the pipe completely, like the washer at the end of the valve stem in a faucet. Notice that if the *float* is lowered, the plunger is raised. This is what happens when the toilet is flushed. The float rests on top of the water. As the water rushes out of the tank, the float falls, raising the plunger. Water is now permitted to flow past the valve and comes out of the *filler tube* and

out of the *refill tube.* The water enters much more slowly than the water rushing out, so that the tank soon empties. When the flush ball in Figure 7-13 closes the opening, water no longer rushes out, and the water entering through the filler tube soon fills up the tank. As the tank fills, the float rises, and the plunger moves downward to close off the water supply. When the float is high enough, the water supply is completely shut off.

The action of the water flushing the toilet is vigorous and may force too much water from the trap in the toilet, so that there is no longer a good seal against sewer gases. To prevent this, it is necessary to add more water to the toilet after the flushing is over. This is done by the refill tube, shown in Figure 7-14, which is directed into the overflow tube shown in Figure 7-13. Thus, after the flush ball has closed off the opening to the toilet, water enters the tank from the filler tube, and at the same time water enters the toilet from the refill tube, by way of the overflow tube. When the float is high enough, both are shut off.

7-11. Toilet Tank Repairs

Most of the troubles in a toilet tank are easy to correct and well within the capabilities of the home owner. Usually you can tell what the difficulty is just from looking into the tank, but if you have a clear understanding of the operation of the flushing and refill mechanisms, you can probably figure out the repair procedure just from the symptoms.

Suppose you turn the handle and the toilet does not flush. One possibility is that the tank is empty. Lift up the top and look into the tank. Be careful not to drop in any small objects that were placed on top of the tank. If there is no water in the tank, someone probably turned off the control valve on the pipe under the tank and forgot to turn it on again. This valve should be turned all the way counter-clockwise to permit water to flow. If the tank *is* full of water, the trouble is in the flushing mechanism. Refer again to Figure 7-13. The trip lever may be broken, the linkage wire may have come loose, or the loop on top of the lift rod may have rusted off. In any of these cases, turning the handle will not lift the flush ball,

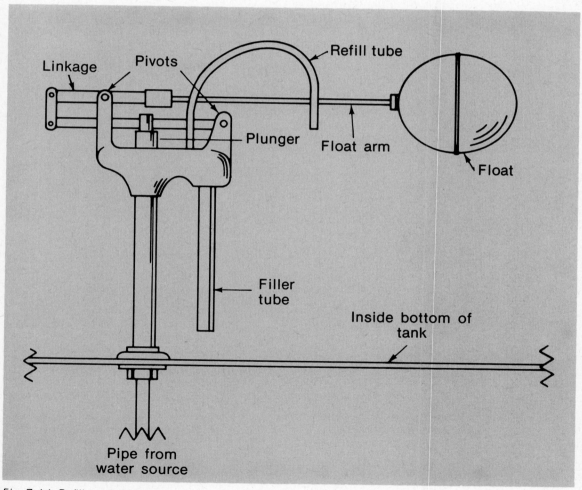

Fig. 7-14. Refill mechanism.

and thus the toilet won't flush. All these parts are available separately at any hardware or plumbing store. As an emergency measure, if you can't get to a hardware store immediately, tie a string to the lift rod and let it hang over the edge of the tank, with the top off. To flush, simply pull up on the string. If the linkage wire is broken, you can *make* another from a piece of stiff wire.

If the toilet continues to run at the end of the flush, the flush ball may not be reseating. This will happen if the lift rod is bent so that it doesn't slide freely in the guide, or if the guide has slipped on the overflow tube so that the ball is no longer directly over the opening in the seat. The ball itself may be eroded by minerals in the water, so that even if it is seated correctly the pits and bumps on the ball prevent a good seal and allow water to continue to leak into the toilet. If the linkage wire is bent or if the ball is eroded, it is best to replace the ball with a new "flapper" type of flush ball. This takes the place of the flush ball, guide, linkage wire and lift rod. It is very simple to install with full directions on the package and is available at most hardware stores. The guide should be loosened on the overflow tube and slipped off and discarded. The new flapper ball has a rubber ring connected to it which slides down over the overflow tube, and a chain connects the ball to the trip lever.

If the flush ball develops a leak so that it loses its buoyancy, you will have to hold the handle down to the end of the flush. To correct this, replace the ball with a flapper ball, as described.

The toilet may continue to run because of a defect in the refill mechanism. This mechanism is called a *ballcock* (refer to Figure 7-14). When the tank has refilled, the float should rise and push the plunger into its opening to stop the water from entering. A sketch of the plunger itself is shown in Figure 7-15. This shows the plunger raised from its seat (the float in the tank would be lowered). The plunger has a packing and O-ring around it to prevent water from emerging from the top. Water enters and flows to the refill and filler tubes. A leather or plastic washer on the bottom of the plunger seals the opening when

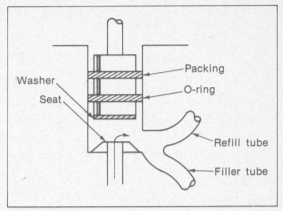

Fig. 7-15. Plunger detail.

the plunger is down. If there is a defect in this system so that water is not shut off by the plunger, the water will rise in the tank above the overflow tube and then will flow through this tube into the toilet.

One possible defect is a worn washer on the plunger. To check this, reach into the tank and raise the float arm slightly with your fingers. If this causes the water to stop flowing, the washer is all right. If not, replace the washer. It is held in place with a brass screw which is easily removed. Take the old washer or the whole plunger with you when you buy a new one to make sure that the new washer fits correctly.

If raising the float arm stops the flow of water, the fault is in the float, the float arm or the linkage. Check the float. It can be unscrewed from the float arm. If it has developed a leak, water will get inside it, and it won't rise enough to push down the plunger. In that case, replace the float. Newer floats are made of plastic instead of metal and last indefinitely. If the float is all right but rises to the top of the tank without shutting off the water, bend the float arm downward so that the plunger will be forced down before the float has risen to the top. Conversely, if the water shuts off too soon, filling only a small part of the tank, bend the float arm the other way to raise the water level before the plunger closes.

If a toilet has not been used for a long time, the pivots and linkage may get stiff and prevent the float arm from closing the plunger properly. You can correct this by applying one or two drops of oil on each pivot and joint, and raising and lowering the float arm a few times to work in the oil.

If a toilet tank leaks at the point where the water pipe enters the tank the fault is usually caused by a worn gasket. With the water shut off, first flush the toilet, and then sponge out any water remaining. Grasp the ballcock (the refill mechanism) inside the tank with one hand to hold it steady, and with the other apply an adjustable wrench to the nut on the pipe under the tank. You will then be able to remove the ballcock and replace the gasket. You can replace the whole ballcock, if you wish, in the same way. Newer ballcocks are almost completely silent in operation.

Climate Control

Air motion and *humidity* affect a person's comfort as much as *temperature.* The heating system in your home should keep the house at the proper temperature and humidity with a minimum of air motion or drafts.

The *normal* temperature of the human body is 98.6° F (37° C), and the body tries to maintain this temperature regardless of the temperature of the surroundings. When we are in motion, the body generates heat and clothing holds this heat in, so that we feel warm even if the outside temperature is much less than 98.6° F. If it is very cold or we do not move enough voluntarily to keep our body temperature up, we start to shiver, and this involuntary motion helps generate more heat. When the surrounding temperature is too high and tends to raise our body temperature above normal, we sweat, and the evaporation of this moisture cools our bodies and helps maintain a constant temperature. If we stand in front of a fan, the flow of air increases the evaporation and thus cools us faster.

A room temperature of 70° F (21.1° C) is generally considered satisfactory, but for you to feel comfortable at this temperature, the humidity must also be correct. *Relative humidity* is the percentage of water vapor in the air compared to the amount of water vapor the air could hold if it were saturated. When the humidity is low, less than 40 per cent,

body moisture evaporates rapidly, and you may feel too cool even at a temperature of 80° F (26.7° C). On the other hand, when the humidity is too high, above 60 per cent, body moisture cannot evaporate easily, and you feel hot and damp at temperatures below 70° F. Also, when the humidity is too high, your house itself suffers from damp walls, and can be damaged from excess moisture in the air. With a temperature near 70° F at about 50 per cent humidity, the average person would feel quite comfortable. Given sufficient money, it might be possible to design and build a climate-control system that could maintain ideal temperature and humidity conditions in every room of a house despite extremes of winter cold and summer heat. However, from a practical standpoint, we are willing to make some small sacrifices in comfort to save large amounts of money, and thus heating systems are not ideal.

Houses may be heated by coal, oil or gas. Electricity is also used in some areas close to large hydroelectric power plants, but in most parts of the country electricity is too expensive for central heating. The fuel is used to heat air or water, and the heat is carried to all parts of the house by hot air, hot water or steam. Each type of burner and heat-carrying system has its own problems.

With a forced-air heating system, the furnace becomes the climate control center of the house.

8-1. Furnaces

Before oil burners were invented, most homes used coal furnaces. Later, in order to take advantage of the "automatic" features of oil heat, many of these coal furnaces were converted to oil by removing the grates and installing oil burners. Automatic coal-burning furnaces were also developed. In newer homes that use oil burners or gas burners, there may be no resemblance between the burner and the old-fashioned coal furnace. Nevertheless, all these burners are referred to as furnaces whether they burn oil, coal or gas.

An automatic furnace of any type is controlled by a *thermostat* which is a temperature-controlled switch, usually located in or near the living room in your home. It has a small lever to set the desired temperature. When the temperature in the room drops slightly below this temperature, the thermostat closes, turning on the furnace. When the room temperature is slightly higher than the setting, the thermostat opens, shutting off the burner. If the thermostat is dirty or worn, it will not operate correctly.

To check a thermostat, remove the cover. If there is dirt inside, use a vacuum cleaner to clean it out. Dirt can get between the contacts and prevent the thermostat from turning on the furnace. When the thermostat is clean, check its operation by moving the control lever over a wide range. You should hear a click as the thermostat makes and breaks contact. Make sure that the wires running to the furnace are firmly attached to their mounting screws. If the thermostat seems defective, unscrew these wires and bring them together. If the furnace starts when the wires are brought together but will not operate otherwise, you need a new thermostat. Remove the old one and ask your hardware dealer for a replacement.

Too much dirt in a thermostat can also cause the contacts to stick together when

Thermostat with cover removed.

they should separate. In this case, the furnace continues to run after the room has reached its proper temperature, and soon the house gets too hot. The thermostat should be cleaned with a vacuum cleaner at least once a year to prevent this. Sticky contacts can be cleaned by pulling a piece of fine sandpaper between them. Do not use emery paper.

Before you assume something is wrong with your furnace, make sure that the main switch is turned on. Too often a home owner has called a repairman for his furnace to discover that the only "trouble" was failure to turn on the main switch after turning if off for maintenance.

If the room in which the thermostat is located reaches its preset temperature before the other rooms are sufficiently warm, the thermostat will open, shutting off the furnace. Outer rooms will be too cool. A possible solution is to locate the thermostat in an outer room, but if you do this, it will not solve the problem of different temperatures in different rooms. The outer rooms will reach the desired temperature, but the room where the thermostat was will be much warmer. You can accomplish the same thing by simply moving the lever on the thermostat to a higher setting. It is almost impossible to *balance* radiators so that all rooms reach the same temperature at the same time. Some hot-water systems have special valves on radiators which can be adjusted to control the heat, and air ducts in hot-air systems can be partially closed, but any adjustment in one room affects the heat in all others. Some trial-and-error experimenting will be necessary, but *moving the thermostat will not solve the problem.*

Gas as a fuel has many advantages over coal or oil. Gas requires no storage tank, whereas with the other fuels you will need a coal bin or an oil tank, either of which takes up space which can be used for other purposes. A gas flame produces much less soot and smoke than either oil or coal and thus is "cleaner". However, in most locations gas is more expensive than either of the other two fuels and may be prohibitively high in extremely cold climates.

Gas burners require almost no attention. When the burner is operating properly, air

Have your gas or oil burner checked periodically by a professional.

mixes with gas in a predetermined ratio and the mixture burns with a blue flame and a yellow tip. If there is no yellow, there is not enough air mixing with the gas, whereas too much yellow indicates that too much air is getting in. If the flame is not correct, look for the air-intake shutter and adjust it until a small tip of yellow appears in the blue flame.

As long as the gas burner shows a proper flame, you can forget about it. However, breakdowns usually occur on the coldest day of winter, and it is better to anticipate and prevent trouble rather than to repair a fault later. Thus, you should have your gas burner checked periodically by your local gas company or a reliable gas-burner repairman. If this is done every three years, your burner should give you many years of service. Your repairman will clean the burner, adjust the flame and look for defective parts. Watch him do it the first time, and you may decide that you can do it yourself later, since it is not a difficult job.

If a gas burner will not work at all, first check to see if the pilot is lit. *Do not smoke while working on a gas burner.* If the pilot is out, it may have been blown out by a strong gust of wind or the gas may have been shut off because of some civil emergency. Before trying to relight the pilot, make sure there is no odor of gas. It is dangerous to light a match if there is gas in the room. The proper procedure is to shut off the gas in the line to the pilot. You will find a valve in the line with a straight handle on it. When this handle is parallel to the gas pipe, the line is open. Close it by turning this handle so that it is perpendicular to the pipe. Now wait about half an hour so that any gas which may have leaked into the room can dissipate. Open the valve again and allow about 15 or 20 seconds for the gas to get to the pilot. Light a match, and, holding it with a pair of pliers, apply it to the tip of the pilot. On some burners there is a red safety button which must be pushed, and there should be a tag indicating the proper procedure to relight the pilot. Look for this tag and follow the instructions. Relighting the pilot should solve the immediate problem, but you

should also look for the cause of the shutdown. If the pilot is located in a drafty place, you should shield it from drafts. If the pilot light is too small, you can increase the amount of gas reaching it by adjusting a small screw in the line. The flame should be about 1″ long at the tip of the opening.

If the pilot light is lit, the thermostat is working and the furnace still won't work, the trouble is probably a defective *thermocouple.* This is a device which generates a voltage when heated, and this voltage is applied to open an electrically-operated valve which allows gas to get to the main burner. With a little care you can replace a thermocouple yourself. The two wires to the valve are attached to screws. Loosen these screws and disconnect the wires. The thermocouple attached to these wires is usually screwed in place with a hexagonal screw or nut. Use an adjustable wrench to loosen it. Replace the unit with a duplicate thermocouple, obtainable in many plumbing shops or service outlets.

Not much can happen to a coal furnace to keep it from operating, but soot can reduce its efficiency. When the furnace is shut down for the summer, it should be thoroughly cleaned.

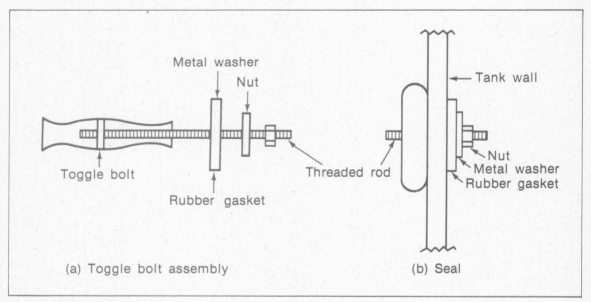

(a) Toggle bolt assembly   (b) Seal

Fig. 8-1. Tank repair.

This central air conditioner features top discharge of condenser air and a high capacity guarded fan.

Besides wasting heat, soot combines with water vapor in the air to form corrosive acids, which can damage the metal parts of the furnace. To clean the furnace, first close all dampers and drafts so that wind blowing down the chimney will not blow loose soot out of the furnace. Use a stiff wire brush to scrape soot off all surfaces exposed to the fire. Then remove the loose soot with a vacuum cleaner with a long hose attachment.

Soot and ashes must be removed from smoke pipes, ash pit and ash cleanout chambers. The pipe may be taken apart and each section cleaned separately. Water and soap or detergent can be used to make the job easier. Before dismantling the smoke pipe, label each section so that you will be able to reassemble the sections in the correct order. When the pipe is reassembled, make sure there are no leaks. Leaks in smoke pipe can be sealed with ordinary asbestos cement applied with a putty knife, trowel or an old kitchen spatula.

Grates in a coal-burning furnace can be coated with ordinary motor oil during the off-season to keep them from rusting. Door hinges should also be oiled. When you refire the furnace in the fall, this oil will burn off harmlessly.

Oil burners should also be cleaned every year in the off-season. Soot should be removed in the same manner as described above for coal furnaces. All surfaces which may rust should be coated with motor oil or household lubricating oil. This oil will burn off when the burner is put back in service in the fall. Shut off the main switch to the burner during the summer, but don't forget to turn it on again when you start the furnace in the fall.

The fuel tank for your oil burner should be filled for the summer to prevent water vapor from causing rust. If the tank is left empty or partially full, water vapor in the air trapped in the tank may condense and cause leaks due to rusting. If a tank develops a leak, you can make a temporary repair (Figure 8-1), using a toggle bolt assembly obtainable in most hardware stores. The unit contains a toggle bolt, rubber gasket, brass washer and nut, mounted on a threaded rod, shown in Figure 8-1(a). The toggle bolt is pushed into the tank through the hole in the wall. You may have to enlarge the hole to do this. Then the nut is tightened on the outside, squeezing the rubber gasket against the side of the tank as in Figure 8-1(b). This makes a good seal. However, any seal of a leak in a tank should be considered *temporary,* since if a leak occurs in one place, there are probably other weak spots which will develop into leaks later. In an emergency, you can close a pinhole leak with ordinary chewing gum.

If the oil burner fails to operate, first make sure there is fuel in the tank. Don't rely on the gauge on the tank, but remove the cover and push a long stick inside to see if there is really fuel there. Gauges frequently become defective. Your next check should be your thermostat, discussed earlier in this section. If you have fuel and your thermostat is in working order, your best bet is to call a service man. You may be able to fix the trouble yourself, but if you make a mistake so that too much oil gets into the furnace before it fires, there could be an explosion. Since this is a dangerous area, it is better to let a professional handle it. In general, it is wise to call in a professional repairman every year when the burner is shut down for the summer. He will clean the furnace (a messy job, anyway) and reset all controls, as well as checking the operation of motors, pumps and filters. A good annual checkup can keep your oil burner operating efficiently and save you a lot of trouble. It is worth the expense.

8-2. Hot-Air Systems

The first central heating plants were hot-air systems similar to that shown in Figure 8-2. The furnace itself burned coal or wood, which was fed into the fire chamber through the firing door. Ashes were removed through a door at the bottom of the furnace. Cold air from outside the house entered the furnace through the cold-air inlet. This fresh air surrounded the fire chamber but never came in contact with the flames. As the air became heated, it expanded and became lighter than

Vacuum hot-air registers occasionally.

the air in the house. Consequently it rose in the hot-air ducts and entered each room through a register set in the floor. As more hot air entered a room, the cooler air already there tended to leak out through cracks in window frames and other minute openings in the building.

As the hot air flows through the hot-air ducts, it loses some of its heat. As a result, rooms farthest from the furnace receive air which is not as warm as the air reaching the nearer rooms. To equalize the heat, dampers are provided in the ducts, and these can be set to block the flow of air to the nearer rooms partially, or, if desired, completely. The flow of hot air in the ducts is also affected by wind outside the house, so that the rooms on the windy side may be cooler than those on the sheltered side. Again, the dampers can be adjusted to compensate for this.

The major disadvantage of this system is that on a very cold day the outside air is many degrees below a comfortable temperature, and this air must be heated above normal room temperature so that it will rise in the hot-air ducts. This requires a hot fire in the furnace and high rate of fuel consumption. In practice, the fire burns continuously in a coal furnace, since starting a new fire when the furnace is dead is an undesirable chore.

A modern forced hot-air system is shown in Figure 8-3. The hot-air ducts, leading from the furnace to the rooms to be heated, feed registers which are located at high points on the walls rather than at floor level. In each room or area a register near the floor feeds to a cold-air return. A blower near the burner draws the cold air in the room back into the heating chamber to be reheated. A filter in the line removes dirt which might damage the blower motor. The filter also cleans the recirculated air. The cold air which returns to

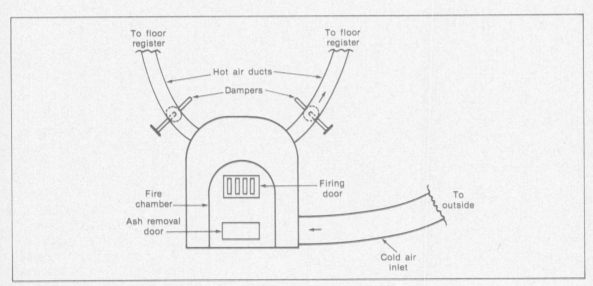

Fig. 8-2. Gravity hot-air system.

A modern room air conditioner such as this has controls that enable the user to maintain an ideal temperature near 70°F.

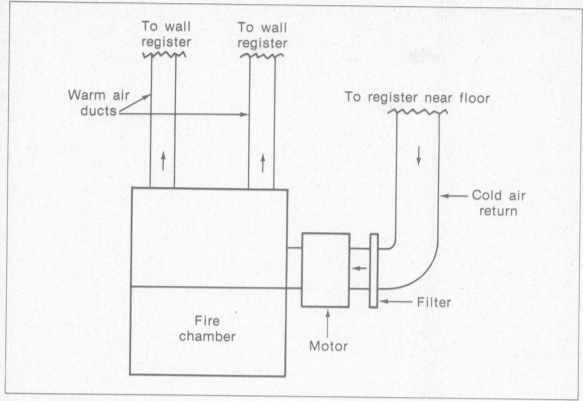

To wall register

To wall register

Warm air ducts

To register near floor

Cold air return

Fire chamber

Filter

Motor

Fig. 8-3. Forced hot-air system.

the furnace may be only a few degrees below room temperature, so that the amount of heat required to bring it up to a suitable temperature is much less than in the gravity system. Although the same air is apparently circulating continuously, some fresh air leaks in from outside through the usual cracks in window and door frames and other openings in the house. This supplies the necessary change of air in the system.

The forced hot-air system is frequently used with a gas burner in moderate climates. The blower motor and burner are both turned on automatically by the thermostat when the room temperature falls below the temperature setting on the control, and both are shut off when the desired temperature is reached. If the burner were to operate without the blower being on, the concentration of heat could be dangerous. To prevent this, control circuits do not allow the burner to ignite until the motor is operating.

There isn't much that can go wrong with the

gravity hot-air system of Figure 8-2. In practice, the furnace usually supplies more heat than is needed, so that if leaks develop in air ducts, the loss of heat would not be noticed. The ducts must slope up from the furnace so that hot air will rise to the registers above. If a duct sags so that part of it has a downward slope, hot air may not pass beyond the peak, with the result that the room fed by the duct will be cold. If a room is cold, check the slope of the duct leading to it, and if necessary, prop it up correctly. A duct can also be blocked by rags and other foreign objects dropped into a register accidentally. When this happens, the duct will be warm up to the blockage and cold above it. Dismantle the duct at the point of trouble and remove the obstruction. Reassemble the duct as it was originally. If dirt rises from the registers, it is a sign that you forgot to clean the ducts. This should be done routinely once a year, as described in Section 2-6, Volume 1.

In both systems, if the ducts are made of

lightweight metal, they will expand as they are heated by the warm air passing through. This expansion can cause creaking noises, which may be objectionable but are not otherwise harmful. The noise can be deadened by placing sponge rubber or felt pads at points where the duct touches the wooden members of the building. Vibrations in the ducts can also cause noise, and this can be cured by making sure the ducts are firmly anchored.

Noisy operation can be caused by trouble other than faults in the ducts. If noise comes from the furnace itself, it is usually caused by vibrations of loose parts. Shut off the burner and look for loose bolts and nuts. Tighten everything inside and out. If noise comes from the blower, the blades of the fan may be rubbing against the frame, or loose cables may be interfering with the blades. Bend the blades, if necessary, or tie any loose cables out of the way. Dirt on the blades can also cause vibrations in the blower. Remove dirt with a vacuum cleaner.

Dirt streaks on walls and ceilings near hot-air registers are signs that air ducts need cleaning. If the air filter is kept clean and changed periodically, this problem should not arise. The cold-air return is a prime source of dust, and this should be cleaned annually by removing the covers on the registers near the floor (in forced-air systems) and vacuuming out all visible dust.

If fuel bills suddenly get high, the trouble may be due to a loose belt on the blower motor, clogged filters or blocked air ducts. If the blower belt is loose or slipping, look for an adjustable pulley to take up the slack. You should be able to move the belt about 1 inch with your finger when it has the correct tension. If it is too tight, it will cause the motor to cut out because of too great a load. If too loose, it slips so that the fan doesn't turn as fast as it should to keep the air circulating. If a pulley is loose on a shaft, it produces the same effect as a loose belt. That is, the blower doesn't rotate as fast as it should. If you see a shaft turning inside its pulley, look for a set screw on the pulley, and tighten it until the pulley is firmly fixed on the shaft. Always check the filter for dirt, and clean if necessary. Filters are cheap, and the cost of replacing

the filter every month during the heating season is negligible. You may prefer to do this rather than try to brush out the accumulated dust.

If too much heat is supplied, check your thermostat. It is possible that someone pushed it to a higher setting. If not, the thermostat may be stuck in the *on* position. Check your thermostat as explained in Section 8-1, and if it is defective, replace it. Too little heat is usually a sign of a blockage in the system, but it can also be caused by a loose belt or pulley or a loose connection at the thermostat.

8-3. Hot-Water Systems

There are two kinds of hot-water heating systems, gravity and forced. A gravity hot-water system is illustrated in Figure 8-4. The fire in the furnace heats water in a boiler to about 170° or 180° F. The hot water, being lighter than the cooler water in the pipes, rises into the radiators above the boiler. From the radiators, heat is given off into the several rooms, and the water becomes about 20° F cooler. The cooler water returns to the boiler by way of the return pipes. Since the water expands when it is heated, an expansion tank, located at the top of the system (usually in the attic), is provided to accommodate the excess water. This tank is usually open to the air and may have an overflow pipe connected to a drain, although with proper operation, the tank should not overflow.

In the forced hot-water system (Figure 8-5), a pump is added to keep the water circulating. The system is completely sealed, including the expansion tank, so that the water is under pressure. This permits heating the water above normal boiling point, and water temperatures may be as high as 250° F. When the system is cold, the expansion tank has some air in it, and this air is compressed as the water expands, thereby increasing the pressure.

Since the water is *pumped* through the system, water leaves the radiators when the

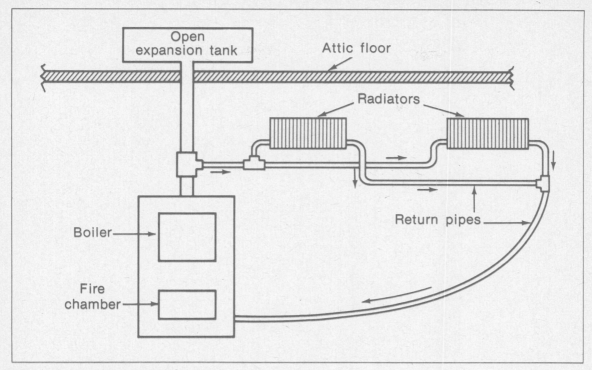

Fig. 8-4. Gravity hot-water system.

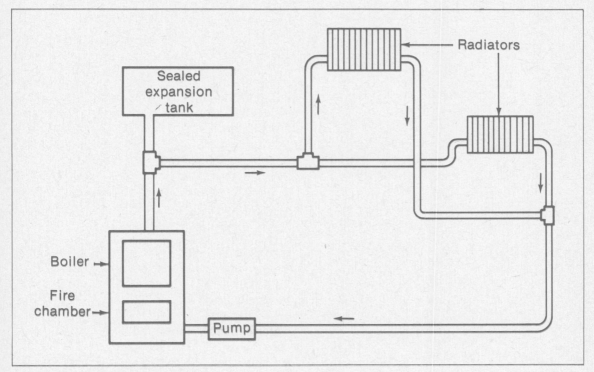

Fig. 8-5. Forced hot-water system.

Both the interior and the drum of a drum-type humidifier are easily accessible for cleaning. Clean often to prevent build-up of mineral deposits.

A dehumidifier runs more efficiently if its condenser coils are vacuumed occasionally.

pump is operating, even if it has not yet given up its heat to the radiators. This happens when the ambient temperature is only slightly below the thermostat setting. Thus, the water returning to the boiler would still be hot, and little fuel would be used to bring it up to a high temperature again. Notice that in the forced system it is not necessary to have the expansion tank above the level of the radiators.

In the gravity system, the main pipes are comparatively large, about 3″ in diameter. In the forced hot-water system, more heat is carried because of the higher temperature and pressure, and thus smaller pipes may be used. The main pipe may be only 1-1/2″ in diameter, and the risers to the radiators may have a diameter as small as 1/2″.

If you keep water in the system and vent the radiators periodically, you should have no trouble with your hot-water system. When you have a serviceman make his annual maintenance checkup, ask him to show you how to add water to the boiler. This is done simply by opening a valve. The proper water level is indicated by a fixed red mark or arrow on a water gauge on the boiler. The actual water level is shown by a movable black arrow on the same gauge. When the black arrow falls below the red mark, you must add water until the two coincide. From five to ten days after you add water, you should vent the radiators, using the technique described in Section 2-6, Volume 1. Some systems have a control which adds water automatically when the level is too low.

The pump and the pump motor both need oiling periodically. If there is an oil cup, add one or two drops of oil once a month, but do not add oil if the cup is full.

Leaks in pipes or fittings in the hot-water heating system are repaired in the same way as leaks in water pipes, described in Section 7-3. Make sure that any patches or compounds used to seal the leaks will stand the higher temperature of the heating system. Most sealing compounds are safe even at the high temperatures of a forced hot-water system, but as a check ask your hardware- or plumbing-supply dealer when you buy the material. When applying a sealing compound or plastic patch, make certain that all surfaces are dry and clean. It is usually necessary to drain the water out of the system above the damaged pipe before tackling the job of fixing a leak. Don't forget to refill the pipes after the leak is repaired.

8-4. Steam Heat

In a steam heat system, water in the boiler is heated to boiling so that it is converted to steam. The steam rises in the pipes faster than hot water or hot air, so that steam heats a cold house more quickly than any other method. A steam system is shown in Figure 8-6. Notice that there is only one pipe connected to each radiator. Steam rises from the boiler and enters the radiators through these pipes. When the radiator is cold, the steam valve on the end opposite to the pipe is open, and air in the radiator is pushed out through the valve as steam comes in at the other end. When all the air is out of the radiator and steam has reached the valve, heat from the steam expands the valve, sealing it. As a result, very little steam escapes.

As the radiators give off heat to warm the house, the steam inside cools and condenses to water. The water flows back to the boiler through the same pipe that brought the steam. Since the water flows back in a trickle, it is possible to have steam rising and water returning in one pipe at the same time. Note, however, that the pipe must slope toward the furnace. If there is a dip in a pipe, water could collect there and block off the pipe to the passage of steam.

A steam boiler has a few attachments which are quite different from anything on a boiler in a hot-water system. Three of these are shown in Figure 8-7. The water gauge in Figure 8-7(a) is on the side of the furnace and shows the water level in the boiler. The top of the water in the glass tube is at the same level as the top of the water in the boiler, so that the water level is easily discernible. The proper level is about midway in the glass tube. Usually, you should fill the boiler so that the glass is about three quarters full, as in Figure

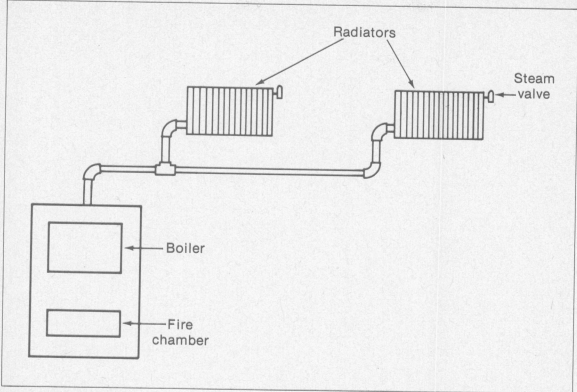

Fig. 8-6. Steam system.

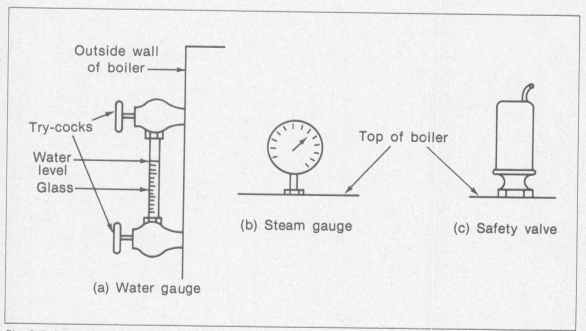

Fig. 8-7. Parts of steam boiler.

Metal weather stripping may be bought in kits and is easily installed by following directions on the package.

8-7(a). As steam is lost from the system, the level will drop, and when the glass is only one quarter full, fill it again to the three-quarter level. There is a cold-water pipe with a valve on it leading to the boiler. Turn the valve counterclockwise to let water enter the boiler, and shut it off when the water is at the correct level.

The steam gauge in Figure 8-7(b) is mounted on top of the boiler and indicates the steam pressure inside the boiler. If everything else is working, this can be ignored. In general, the pressure should not exceed 15 pounds per square inch. Since you cannot be expected to watch the pressure gauge 24 hours a day, a safety valve is also mounted on top of the boiler, illustrated in Figure 8-7(c). This valve pops open automatically when the pressure exceeds the safe limit and permits steam to escape until a safe pressure is reached, then it closes. Since the valve may not open for several months or even years as long as everything is working properly, you may have a nasty suspicion that it may not operate when required. Thus, for most valves a test lever is provided so that its operation can be checked. Make it a point to test the operation of the valve a few times during the heating season. If the valve is defective,

replace the whole unit. With the furnace off and the boiler cool, unscrew the valve, using a pipe wrench or adjustable wrench on the hexagonal section. The valve is threaded so that it comes off easily, and a new one can be screwed into the opening.

Leaks in steam pipes or at joints can be fixed in the same manner as leaks in water pipes, as described in Section 7-3. Make sure that all surfaces are clean and dry. Most sealing materials will withstand the temperatures of steam pipes, but, to make sure, check with your hardware dealer when you buy the material.

If one radiator remains cool when the rest heat up, steam is not reaching that radiator. Check to see that the valve at the input end (where the pipe enters) is open. Someone may have closed it accidentally. The valve should be turned completely counterclockwise to open it. If the steam valve on the radiator is defective, it may not permit air to escape, thereby preventing steam from entering the radiators. To check this, remove the steam valve completely. If the radiator now fills with steam (when the furnace is going), the steam valve is at fault. Close the input valve before too much steam enters the room. The steam valve can be cleaned in kerosene

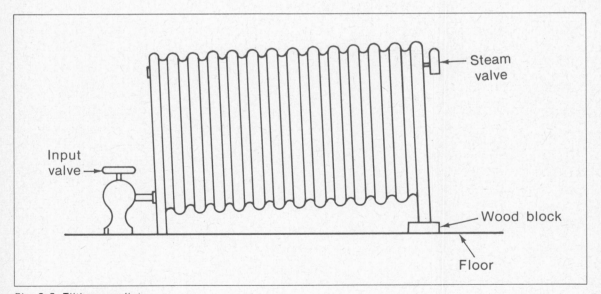

Fig. 8-8. Tilting a radiator.

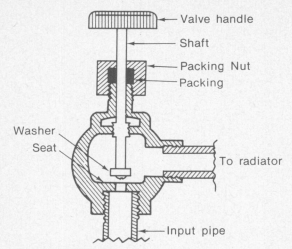

Fig. 8-9. Radiator valve.

or a strong solution of trisodium phosphate (TSP) and water, or, if too badly dirty, can be replaced with a new valve, which is quite inexpensive.

If the radiator still won't get hot, there may be a water block in the line or in the radiator itself. The radiator should slope toward the input pipe so that water condensing inside flows back to the boiler. If water remains in the radiator, the system will be noisy, and if enough water remains, it may block the entrance of steam. Radiators may tilt in the wrong direction because of sagging floors. To correct this, put small blocks of wood under the feet of the radiator farthest from the input pipe (Figure 8-8). If the floor or structure has sagged so that the main pipe slopes in the wrong direction, put blocks under all four feet of the radiator to pull up the pipe and make it slope toward the boiler.

If water leaks at the input valve, it is usually because of worn packing. A typical valve is shown in Figure 8-9. Water or steam is prevented from coming out of the tip of the valve by packing held tightly against the shaft. If this packing material gets worn, it no longer makes an effective seal. Sometimes you can compress it sufficiently by tightening the packing nut with an adjustable wrench, but if this doesn't work you will have to put in new packing. To remove and replace it, first make sure the radiator is cool and then remove the

valve handle by unscrewing a screw in the center. Remove the packing nut with an adjustable wrench and slide it up and off the shaft. The old packing will come with it. Remove the old packing with an ice pick or screwdriver, and wind new packing material into the packing nut around the shaft. Packing looks like graphite-impregnated string and is obtainable at any hardware store. When you put in new packing, wind it in a clockwise direction so that it will compress when the packing nut is tightened.

Valves in hot-water radiators may leak for the same reason and in the same manner. The solution is the same, except that the radiator must be drained first. This means that the whole system must be drained until the water is below the level of the radiator valve that needs new packing. After replacing the packing, refill the water system before firing the boiler.

Valves on steam radiators should be either all the way open or all the way closed. In water radiators, however, valves can be left partially open as a means of regulating the amount of hot water coming in. In this way, you can cut down the heat in radiators that are too hot.

8-5. Radiant Heat

Instead of radiators or hot-air registers, heating units can be placed in floors, walls or ceilings. In such a system, the heating unit warms the air by radiation so that you feel as comfortable and warm with air temperatures of 65° F as you would in a room heated to 70° F by other methods. In a typical radiant heating system, copper tubing is placed just below the floor. In ranch-type houses on a concrete slab, the copper tubing is embedded in the concrete. A standard hot water furnace heats water to somewhere between 100° to 120° F (about 38° to 50° C), and this warm water is circulated through the copper tubing. This system of heating is very economical after the initial installation, because the water has to be only moderately warm. It is amazingly comfortable, because floors are warm to the touch, and there are no cold spots in the room. In areas where electricity is not too expensive, electrical cables may be used instead of copper tubing and water.

In the hot-water radiant system, the furnace requires the same attention as the furnace in a conventional hot-water system, but no other maintenance is required. The electric system requires no maintenance whatsoever and will work without attention as long as electricity is available. A disadvantage of radiant heating is that carpets lower the efficiency, and for the best results floors should be bare.

8-6. Insulation

The purpose of insulation is to keep heat where it is supposed to be. Insulation holds heat in your house in the winter and prevents heat from getting in during the summer. In addition to making your home more comfortable all year round, insulation helps you save on fuel bills. In areas that experience subzero temperatures during much of the winter, the savings on fuel bills will pay for the cost of insulation in less than two heating seasons. In areas that have winters with frequent temperatures between 0° and 30° F, it may take three years to save enough on fuel to pay for insulating. Even in the warm parts of the country, fuel savings will pay for insulation, although it may take more than five years to amortize the cost.

If your home is already completely insulated, you need do nothing further about this problem. Insulation does not age, and although it may lose some of its effectiveness in time, you could not improve the situation enough, either in comfort or in fuel savings, to

Types of insulation.

justify replacing it or adding to it. If your home is not insulated or only partially insulated, you should consider adding insulation, especially in cold climates. You can do much of the work yourself, although you might want to call in professionals to do a thorough job on exterior walls, where special equipment is required.

Insulating material is available in a variety of forms and materials. Most work on the principle that air is trapped in the spaces between particles or layers of the material, and this "dead" air is a poor conductor of heat. Other types use aluminum foil as a reflector in combination with other materials. The aluminum foil keeps heat out of the house in summer by reflecting it back outside. In general, aluminum alone is not enough to retain heat inside the house in winter, although it is useful in tropical climates to keep houses cool. When aluminum is attached to other insulating material, the combination can be very effective, but it is also very expensive. In general, the handyman should not use reflective materials for insulation.

An important consideration in selecting an insulation material is the effect of moisture in the air. As warm air in the house comes in contact with cool outside walls or windows, water vapor in the air condenses on the cool surface. This is especially noticed as a mist on cold windowpanes, but this condensation is also present on the inside surface of cold outside walls. When insulating material is inside the outside wall, moisture condenses on the inside surface of the insulation, which is inside the wall, because this surface is cooler than the room temperature. If the moisture works its way into the insulation, the wet material then acts as a heat conductor rather than an insulator, since water conducts heat better than air. In other words, *wet* insulation is worthless. To prevent moisture from seeping into the insulation, a *vapor barrier* should be provided. This is simply a layer of nonporous paper, plastic or aluminum foil on the inside surface of the insulating material. Good insulating materials have a vapor barrier attached. When mounting the material, it is important to have the vapor barrier toward the inside of the house (Figure 8-10). If moisture condenses on the vapor

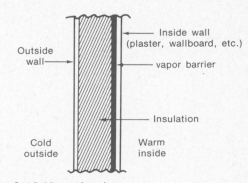

Fig. 8-10. Vapor barrier.

barrier, it cannot get through and eventually evaporates back into the room. The insulation remains dry.

One type of insulating material is *loose fill.* This is the only material that can be used to insulate a wall of a house that is already built, without ripping off panels or plaster. The material consists of small particles of mineral wool, wood fiber or vermiculite (a form of mica). In unfinished attics it can be poured out of bags between the joists in the floor. In walls of existing houses, special equipment is required to blow the insulation into the crevices. Mineral wool is relatively inexpensive, but can irritate the skin if it is handled too much. Since no vapor barrier is provided with loose fills, you must first place a layer of building paper between the joints in the attic floor, and then the loose fill can be simply poured over the paper. Make sure the sheets of paper overlap so that there are no gaps where moisture can get through to the insulation. The depth of insulation should be at least 2″. The thicker the insulation, the less heat loss there will be, and thus the greater will be the fuel savings, but beyond 3″ the savings in fuel will not pay for the extra material.

Insulating panels are wallboards with built-in insulation. Although they are not effective for cold climates, they are sometimes used on walls and ceilings of an extra room added in the cellar or to wall off a garage to make it into a spare room. These panels are available in decorative designs, so that they simplify construction of the new room. No paint or papering is required. However, this material should be used only in moderate climates and only for the "extra" room.

Flexible insulation is available in *blankets*, which are long rolls, and *batts*, which are usually 4′ or 8′ long. These may be of mineral wool, wood fibers or fiberglass, and come in 1″ to 6″ thicknesses. The standard width just fits between studs spaced 16″ apart, and extra-wide batts are also available. If you use batts or blankets, buy material with a vapor barrier already attached. Flameproof blankets are more expensive but may be worth the investment.

Blankets are probably the most efficient of the insulating materials. Use a thickness of 2″ to 4″. Above 4″ the additional fuel saving is negligible, and below 2″ the material is not effective. You will need a special tool — *a stapling gun* — to install blankets or batts. You could use a hammer to nail the material in

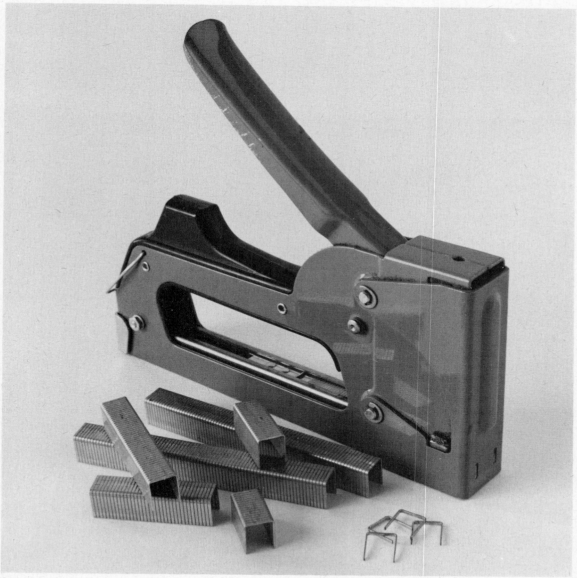

Stapling gun.

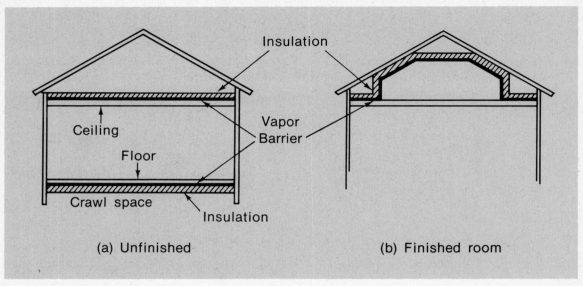

Fig. 8-11. Attic insulation.

place, but a stapler is much faster and easier to use. A stapling gun is not very expensive, and you will probably find many uses for it, such as installing seat covers in your car. If you don't want to buy one, many stores that sell insulation, including the large mail-order houses, will let you borrow a stapling gun if you buy insulation and staples. You have to leave a deposit on the stapler, but you get your money back when you return it. Installing flexible insulation is very easy. Place the material between the studs and drive staples into the studs through the double layer of paper. Staples should be put in every 10″ to 12″ in vertical studs but can be spaced about 18″ when the batt is placed between joints in an attic floor. Be sure the vapor barrier is towards the *inside* of the house, and also make certain that the vapor barrier is continuous by having the edges of one blanket overlap the next.

It would be nice to insulate your whole house, but you can save noticeably on fuel just by insulating your attic. The proper places for attic insulation are shown in Figure 8-11. In Figure 8-11(a), the attic is unfinished, and there is no need for heating it. The insulation is placed on the floor of the attic (over the ceiling of the room below) with the vapor

barrier *toward* the heated room. In this figure, a crawl space is also shown, and if you can get under the house, you can staple batts or a blanket under the first floor also, again making sure the vapor barrier is toward the heated room. In Figure 8-11(b), the attic has a finished room, and the insulation must be carried around the room as shown. Again, the vapor barrier is toward the inside of the house.

8-7. Storm Windows and Doors

In cold weather, the wall of a room next to the outside of your house is usually colder than an inside wall. This wall cools the air next to it, and since cold air is heavier than warm, the cool air moves down toward the floor and warmer air moves across the room to fill the void. If your house is insulated, the dead air space in the outside wall will keep this wall of the room warmer and the air motion will not be as great. That is, it would not be as great except that the cold windowpanes create the same effect. Air is cooled by the cold pane and sinks toward the floor. Warmer air moves toward the window and in turn is cooled. It, too, moves toward the floor, pushing the air there away from the window. The result is that the air is in constant motion, away from the window at floor level, and toward the window in the upper half of the room. Therefore, you feel a draft coming from the window, and if you are like most home owners, you attribute the cause of the draft to air blowing in through a crack in the frame or between the sashes. The truth is this draft occurs from the normal air motion, even if every opening is tightly sealed.

If there were a dead-air space in the window as there is in an insulated wall, the inside pane would not be as cold, and the air motion, and thus draft, would be greatly reduced. The answer is storm sashes or storm windows. A storm window is simply an extra sash containing windowpanes, which is placed over the window, usually outside, so that a dead-air space exists between the storm sash and the window. Anything that creates the dead-air space will work to reduce drafts and incidentally save fuel by preventing heat from leaking out through the windows. You could, for example, simply place a sheet of plywood over the window, but then you would not be able to see through. Storm windows should be transparent.

The cheapest method of creating the desired dead-air space is to tack or tape a sheet of transparent plastic over the window frame *inside the house*. This may not be elegant, but it is effective, with only a little reduction in transparency. Materials for this purpose are sold by mail-order houses and most building-supply stores.

If you live in a cold climate, you should have storm windows, both for added comfort and fuel savings. If your home has none, you will have to make them yourself or have them made, since it is unlikely that your local building-supply house carries storm windows. It would be impossible to stock the wide variety of sizes needed. Making the storm sashes is not difficult, and materials are available in kit form for wooden and aluminum sashes. Measure your window frames carefully on the outside where the storm window will fit. The simplest arrangement is to have the storm sash held by two hangers at the top of the frame and hooked inside at the bottom. In this way the dimensions are not critical and you may even find some second-hand storm sashes that can be used. For a neater appearance, you might want to tailor the sash to the window opening, but this is more difficult. In any case, once you've determined the dimensions, follow the directions in the kit. No special tools are required. Aluminum frames are cut with a hacksaw or any fine-toothed saw. Remove all burrs after sawing by filing smooth.

If possible, storm windows should be designed so that they can be installed from inside the house. It is difficult and dangerous to have to carry sashes up a ladder to mount them. The sash must be small enough and light enough so that you can maneuver it through an open window and mount it on its hangers from inside the house. This is not as important a consideration in one-storey bungalows.

It is possible to buy combination windows which contain both screens and storm sashes. These are mounted permanently and are self-storing. That is, both the screen and storm sash are always contained in the window, but each is moved to the proper position as required. The storm sash is in place during the winter, and the screen in the summer. These combination windows have a higher initial cost than separate screens and storm sashes, but they require less maintenance and last longer because of less handling. If combinations are installed, the home owner is freed from the tasks of installing and removing storm sashes and screens.

When you buy glass for your storm windows, ask to have it cut to size. It should be 1/16″ to 1/8″ smaller than the opening in each direction. Usually there is no extra charge for cutting glass, but even a small nominal charge is worth paying to save yourself the trouble. The installation of glass in doors and windows is described in Section 3-1.

If your storm sash fits snugly in an opening in the window frame, it is more difficult to install if the frame is distorted because of settling of the house. The type that fits against the window frame is not subject to this difficulty. In either case, the storm sash should fit tightly so that air cannot circulate freely from outside into space between the storm sash and the regular house window. If spaces or cracks are visible, close them with weather stripping, as described in the next section.

Wooden sashes should be painted to prevent the wood from absorbing moisture which can distort the sash. However, too much paint may affect the fit of the sash in the frame and should be avoided. In general, paint only when the bare wood can be seen or the paint is so thin that you think it won't last the season. Aluminum sashes don't require paint, but you may want to clean off oxides occasionally. Special cleaning compounds for aluminum sashes are available in most hardware stores.

A storm door creates a dead-air space for a door just as a storm sash does for a window. If you have storm doors, use them, but the fuel savings may be small because not much heat is lost through a door that is well weather-stripped. If the outside door opens on an entryway and there is another door leading into the house, the entryway acts as a dead-air space and reduces drafts when both doors are closed. If there is no entryway, a storm door can be effective in reducing drafts.

If the outside door of the house has a window in it, then the storm door should have a window located at the same level, but if the outside door is solid, the storm door should also be solid. The window in a storm door is usually made of glass, but plastic sheeting can also be used. An excellent material is plastic reinforced with wire mesh. It is much lighter than glass and is shatterproof.

8-8. Weather Stripping

Windows and doors must fit loosely enough so that they can be opened and closed without too much effort. Thus, there is always a crack around each window and door through which heat can escape or cold air can blow in. Even if your home is insulated and furnished with storm windows, the cracks and openings add up to a large source of heat loss. Sealing these cracks will result in additional fuel savings, as well as increased comfort. Weather stripping around windows and doors to seal the crack can result in savings of as much as 20 per cent in fuel costs.

There are many types of weather stripping, and they all work well. Years ago, before special weather-stripping materials were manufactured, home owners frequently rolled up newspaper and fastened the rolls over the openings around the windows and at the bottom of doors. This worked, too, and was probably just as effective as the special materials sold for the purpose today. Materials come in rolls or rigid strips and include felt, foam rubber, plastic, wood and metal, as well as such combinations as felt with a metal backing or plastic tubing with a sponge-rubber core. In new buildings, metal weather stripping is usually included in all double-hung windows and is concealed between the edge of the sash and the frame. If your home does not have weather stripping, you can buy kits of the metal material and install it yourself according to directions, and the result will be an effective and unobtrusive weather stripping. However, it is more expensive than other materials and it requires much more work to install.

If you are concerned with costs and not too concerned about having the weather stripping show, you should shop for the flexible materials such as felt, plastic or foam rubber. Some of these are available with adhesive backing, so that they can be installed with very little effort and no tools, except a pair of scissors or a knife to cut the material to the right length. If you buy material without the adhesive backing, you will have to tack it in place. Tacks should be spaced about 4″ apart.

When you apply weather stripping to a double-hung window, you must seal all the cracks. Attach the material to the frame so that it presses against the window sash, at the sides and bottom of the bottom sash, and at the sides and top of the top sash. Also attach a strip to the bottom sash so that it overlaps the crack between the two sashes. Alternatively, the material could be fastened to the sashes, pressing against the frame, but usually the material is fastened to the fixed portion of the window and presses against the movable part. If the material is mounted correctly, it will be slightly compressed, but it will not be so tight that the window cannot be opened. For metal windows you must use material with an adhesive backing, but for wooden sashes, you can fasten the material either with tacks or adhesive.

For metal casement windows, you can use any of the adhesive-backed weather-stripping materials. There are also special plastic or metal materials, specifically for casement windows, made with a channel which is held on the window only by friction. These are the easiest to install.

Weather stripping for doors utilizes similar principles. The material can be attached to the door or the frame but must close the cracks when the door is closed. Since a door is opened more often than a window in winter, the weather stripping on doors takes more punishment than that on windows, so a long-lasting material should be used. Check with your building supplier or hardware dealer on the qualities of the materials available.

Rain and snow blowing in around cracks in the door, especially at the bottom, can damage the door, even if it is weather-stripped. The edges of the door should be painted often as mentioned in Section 3-3, Volume 1, and a drip cap should be installed.

As a house settles, cracks may appear which permit heat to escape or cold breezes to blow in. Look for these openings and seal them before cold weather arrives. Some of the more common faults occur around door and window frames, at junctions of floors and walls, around pipes entering through floors or walls, and between floorboards in old-fashioned floors. Openings around door or window frames should be caulked as should all openings between two different materials, such as between wood and masonry, metal and masonry, or wood and metal.

When your house was built, caulking was probably installed at every point where two different materials met, such as between the masonry and the rest of the house and between metal flashings and other roofing material. The caulking compounds harden and crack in time and have to be renewed. Caulking compound is a putty-like material which sticks to wood, stone, metal and other building materials, and is available in a variety of colors. When it sets, it remains elastic so that it absorbs different rates of expansion of the surrounding building materials. It can be purchased in tubes and is squeezed out like toothpaste or in long rolls like spaghetti. It is also available in bulk and in disposable cartridges which are used with a caulking gun. Most caulking compounds can be painted. For small openings you can use the roll type and apply it with your fingers or squeeze the compound from a tube. For large openings you should use a caulking gun, which you can usually borrow from the store that sells you the caulking compound. Make sure the surfaces are clean and dry and that all old, dry, caulking material is scraped out. If a hole is very deep, stuff it with a fiber filler such as oakum to about 1″ from the top before adding the caulking compound.

When a house is built, there are certain to be gaps because dimensions are not precise. Thus, floors and walls do not meet exactly. To cover cracks between floor and walls, a piece of molding called a *shoe mold*, is nailed to the wall all around the room at floor level. As a house settles, molding may loosen, opening cracks to heat loss. If you see a shoe molding raised slightly from the floor, you should nail it down again. Hold the molding flush against the floor and nail it to the wall with finishing nails. If it is a small molding, you may drive the nails into the floor. If the molding is distorted, pry it loose with a chisel and replace it, or renail it flush with the floor.

When a pipe passes through a hole in the wall or floor, there is usually space around the pipe, which permits cold air or heat to pass through. This space is usually covered with a decorative flange to conceal the hole, but the flange does not prevent heat loss. You can seal the hole with putty, caulking compound or any sealing material. If the pipe gets hot from hot water or steam, use a sealer that will withstand the temperature.

In old-fashioned houses, flooring was a single layer of boards butting against each other. These boards shrink with age and leave cracks in the floor. Again, you can use any sealer to fill the cracks. One inexpensive but effective method is to sweep sawdust into the cracks and then pour shellac over the sawdust. As the shellac hardens, it makes a good seal.

8-9. Attic Fans

Your attic gets very hot in summer, and rooms just below the attic receive some of this heat. On a hot sunny day the temperature in the attic can be 125° − 130° F and in the rooms just below the attic, 100° F. When a fan is installed to suck the hot air out of the attic, the attic temperature can be lowered quite close to the outside temperature, and the rooms just below do not get nearly as hot.

For a simple installation, place the fan in an attic window pointing outward so that it sucks the hot air out and pushes it outside. Doors to the attic from the rest of the house should be kept open so that hot air throughout the house is pulled up to the attic and forced outside. The fan should fit snugly in the window frame or into a board mounted in the frame. In choosing a fan, first determine the volume of air in the house approximately by adding the volumes of the rooms. Then select a fan that can move that much air in about one minute. If you want to cool only a few rooms, add the volumes of only these rooms, and keep the rest of the house shut off from these rooms simply by closing doors. Of course, the rooms to be cooled must be connected to the attic by open passageways. If your house has insulation and an unfinished attic, a fan is unnecessary. However, the attic will still get hot, and to prevent a build-up of heat, the attic should be ventilated by having openings to the outside at opposite ends. The openings can be open windows or louvers. In either case, the openings should be screened to prevent insects and birds from entering and nesting in the house.

Electricity

There is nothing very difficult about electrical work around the house, but you may not be allowed to do some of the jobs, even though you are perfectly capable of doing adequate work. Local electrical codes will restrict you in many repair jobs, and for a good reason. It seems so easy to string up wires to carry electricity that many people simply do it themselves without bothering about local restrictions. Unfortunately, too often a do-it-yourself electrician uses wire which is too small for the load or strings the wire improperly, and a fire starts. To minimize the risk of fire, almost all cities require new electrical work to be inspected and approved by a city inspector. Some cities even insist that all new installations be done by a licensed electrician. It is unwise to try to install new electrical work without having an inspection, because if you then have a fire in your house, even though caused by something else, your insurance policy may not cover the damage if the illegal wiring is discovered.

You can make simple electrical repairs which involve no changes in wiring. Thus, you can replace a defective switch or outlet, you can fix or replace a broken doorbell, or you can replace an old light fixture with one of modern design. In general, if the repair entails no changes in the house wiring, don't be afraid to tackle it yourself.

Repairs that require changes in the house wiring are best left to a licensed electrician.

This occurs usually when an extra room is added but can also arise if you wish to add a wall switch for a light fixture which has a pull chain. If you wish to make any changes yourself, first consult the city inspector to find out the requirements of the local electrical codes, then comply with these requirements, and, finally, have the work inspected and approved.

If you are not familiar with electricity, it can seem quite mysterious. You don't have to be an engineer to make repairs. In fact, you can replace defective items without knowing anything about how they work, but if you know how things work, repairing is easier and may even be enjoyable. You should learn at least the basic principles explained in Section 9-1.

9-1. Fundamentals

To get a better understanding of electricity, it is useful to compare it to the water system in a household. Water reaches the home through large pipes or mains and is under pressure so that it will be forced out of an open faucet, which may be many feet higher than the water main. When a tap is opened, a current of water flows in the pipe from the main to the tap. The velocity of the current depends on the diameter of the pipe and also on its smoothness. In general, the larger the diameter and the smoother the pipe, the faster will be the flow of current. However, there is a limit determined by the pressure in the main. Electricity is quite analogous. The water main is replaced by the electric power lines which lead to the house. The electricity is under "pressure". This pressure is called *electromotive force (EMF)* and is measured in *volts*. When a suitable connection is made to an electrical appliance, current flows, and the speed of this current depends on factors akin to the smoothness and diameter of the water pipe. In general, the larger the diameter of the wire, the faster will be the electric current. The conductivity of the metal used to make the wire is similar to the smoothness of the water pipe. Some metals, such as copper and silver, are excellent conductors. These are said to have low *resistance*, and current flows through copper, for example, much faster than through iron. Nickel and tungsten are typically poorer conductors which tend to slow down the current. The velocity of electrical current is measured in *amperes*.

Assume that a long garden hose is connected to a water faucet. The pressure may be 80 pounds per square inch. If the hose has an inside diameter of about 1″ and is quite smooth on the inside, water will flow through it rapidly when the faucet is opened wide.

However, if the hose is only 1/4″ in diameter and is not smooth, the flow will be restricted. If a larger hose is connected to the open end of the 1/4″ hose, the water will not move faster through this added hose, since the velocity of flow is limited by the smaller hose. In the same way, if electric current flows through several conductors sequentially, the velocity of the current is limited by the total resistance in the circuit.

In one sense, the analogy between electricity and water breaks down completely. If a water faucet is opened, water pours out. But electricity does not pour out of a wall outlet or an empty lamp socket even when the switch is turned on. Thus, electricity or electric current flows only in a *complete circuit*. This is illustrated in Figures 9-1 and 9-2. At a power station a difference in *electrical potential*, or *e.m.f.*, or voltage is generated. Two wires run from the power station to every house receiving electricity, (Figure 9-1). These wires go through a distribution center in each home and then to the various electrical outlets, such as wall receptacles. In effect, then, each wall receptacle has two terminations which are connected all the way back to the power station or voltage source (Figure 9-2). When an appliance or lamp is plugged into the receptacle, the circuit is completed and current flows, as in Figure 9-2(a). The wiggly

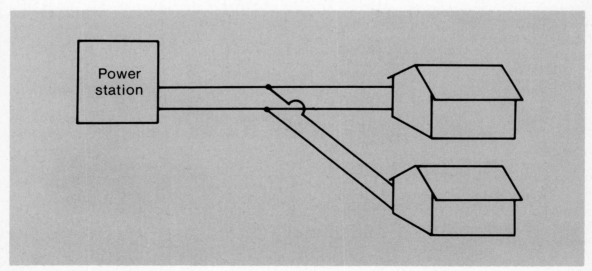

Fig. 9-1. Power distribution.

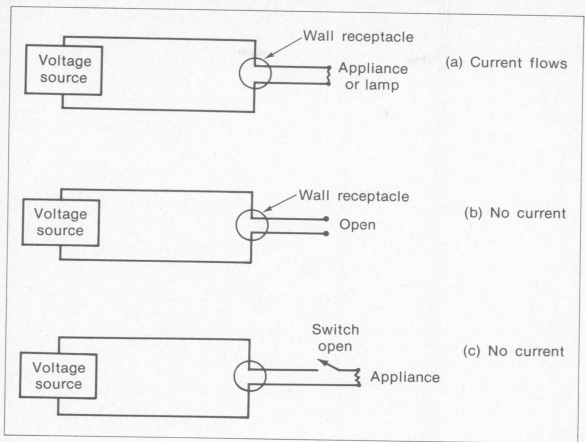

Fig. 9-2. Circuits.

line labeled "appliance or lamp" is the standard electrical symbol for a resistance and is used here to represent the electrical resistance of the appliance. In Figure 9-2(b), the receptacle has nothing plugged into it, thus no current flows, since the circuit is incomplete. Similarly, in Figure 9-2(c), an appliance is plugged into the receptacle, but its switch is in the *off* position. Again, the circuit is incomplete, and no current flows.

The difference in potential, that is, the voltage, between the two terminals in a receptacle is what pushes electricity through a circuit. The two wires or terminals together form a *line*, and each wire by itself is referred to as a *side of the line*. In practice, for safety reasons (explained in the next section) and for simplicity and economy of installation, one side of the line is grounded. That is, it is

physically attached to the earth. This side is then called the *grounded* side of the line, and the other side is the *hot* side. This means that a voltage exists between the hot side and anything else that is physically attached to the earth. In a home, the cold-water pipes are also *grounded*, that is, attached to earth, and thus a voltage exists between the hot side of the line and the cold-water pipes. This is illustrated in Figure 9-3. The plug is removed from the line cord leading to a socket containing a bulb, such as in a table lamp. One wire is attached to the hot side of a receptacle and the other to a faucet or water pipe. The bulb lights. If the wire at the receptacle is moved from the hot side to the ground side, the bulb will not light. Thus, the arrangement shown in Figure 9-3 can also be used to determine which side of the line or receptacle is hot and

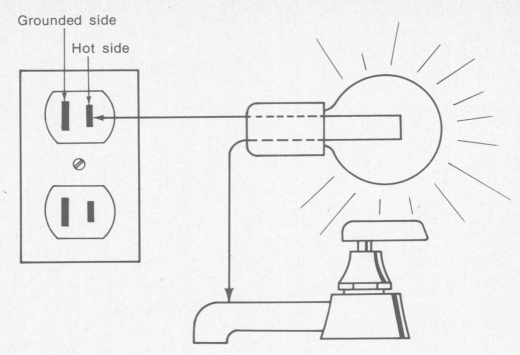

Fig. 9-3. Ground connection.

which is grounded. Similarly, if you touch the hot side of a line and a ground, such as a water pipe, you will get a shock; but you will not get a shock from touching the ground side of the line and another grounded object. You will *not* get a shock even if you touch the hot side, as long as you do not complete the circuit by touching anything else that is grounded. This means you must not be standing on ground or on a damp floor. This explains why birds can sit on high voltage wires; they do not complete the electric circuit.

If you look carefully at a wall receptacle, you will notice that one of the two slots for a plug is longer than the other (Figure 9-4). It is common practice to connect the longer slot to the grounded side of the line, as indicated in the figure. The screw in the center, holding the mounting plate to the wall, is also grounded in most installations. Although the slots are of different lengths, the plugs on most lamps and appliances have prongs which are the same width. Thus, a plug can be inserted to connect either side of the appliance line to either side of the house line.

In industrial appliances, for safety reasons it is desirable to attach the case of the appliance firmly to ground. This is usually done by using a three-pronged plug and a special receptacle. The receptacle has a third hole which is round and connected directly to ground (Figure 9-5). A wire from the case of the appliance is connected to the round prong on the plug so that the case is grounded when the appliance is plugged into the receptacle.

When the electrical current flows through a resistance, it is converted to some other form of energy. This may be heat, light or mechanical motion, or some combination of these. Thus, when current flows through the filament in an electric bulb, it is converted to light, and when current flows through the heating element in a toaster, it is converted to heat. However, the bulb also gets hot, and the heating element glows. That is, in both of these examples, and in every electrical apparatus, some of the electrical energy is converted to unwanted heat or light.

The unit of electrical current is the ampere. This is a unit of velocity indicating flow of electrical charges per second, just as water

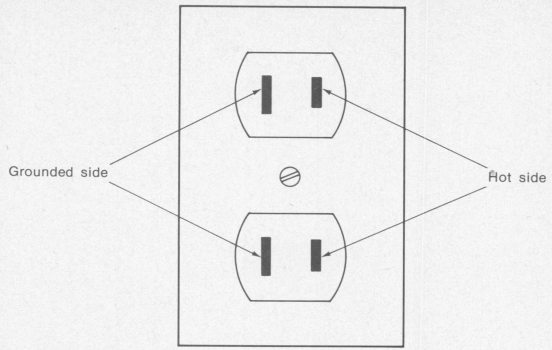

Fig. 9-4. Wall receptacle.

Grounded side

Hot side

current is measured in feet per second. The amount of electrical *power* consumed by an appliance is measured in *watts*. For appliances which produce light or heat, the power consumed in watts is equal to the *product* of the *current* times the *voltage*. For example, one model of electric toaster is rated at 115 volts, 1320 watts. This means that in operation the toaster will draw 1320/115=11.5 amperes. Appliances which have motors that produce motion usually use less power than the product of current times voltage. For example, one model of juicer draws 1.75 amperes at 115 volts. The product is 201.25, but the juicer actually uses only 125 watts.

You pay for electrical energy on the basis of the amount of power used and the time it is used. The unit is a *kilowatt-hour (KWH)*. A kilowatt is 1000 watts and kilowatt-hours are the product of kilowatts and hours. Thus, if you used the 1320-watt toaster for 1/4 hour and the 125-watt juicer for 1/5 hour, you would use 1/4 × 1320 plus 1/5 × 125, or 330 + 25 = 355 watt-hours = 0.355 KWH. Note that if a 50-watt bulb is left on for 10 hours, it uses only 1/2 KWH.

Fig. 9-5. Wall receptacle with ground connection.

When electric current flows through copper wire, there is some power dissipated, even though the wire is an excellent conductor with very low resistance. The greater the current for a fixed diameter of wire, the greater will be the power absorbed by the wire. This power loss becomes evident as heat. When the current through a wire becomes too great, the heat generated may burn the insulation and cause a fire. The safe current-handling capacity of a copper wire depends on the diameter of the wire. Thus, the choice of wire size, not only for house wiring but also for line cords for individual appliances, is affected by the expected current.

The electrical system in a home consists of a service line from the main power lines to the house, a distribution box where the service line divides into many branch lines going to separate rooms, and finally the receptacles and sockets to which the electric appliances are connected. The usual voltage for most electrical appliances is nominally 115 volts, although they will work well at any value between 110 and 120 volts. However, some modern high-power appliances, such as electric ranges and electric clothes dryers, require twice this value to furnish enough power to supply sufficient heat. (Recall that the power is the product of volts times amperes.) To supply both 115 volts and 230 volts, a three-wire service line connects the main power line to the house. This line, shown in Figure 9-6, has one wire grounded, and each of the other wires is at a potential of 115 volts. Alternating current is used, and the voltages on the two hot lines are out-of-phase. This means that when one is 115 volts above ground, the other is 115 volts below, and the difference between them is 230 volts. This last voltage is used to operate ranges, clothes dryers and other high-voltage appliances, while small appliances are operated between either hot wire and ground.

Before considering the current requirements of house wiring, it is necessary to know what current is drawn by each appliance. Typical values of current for various appliances are shown in Table 9-1. Individual appliances may have slightly different requirements, but, in general, those appliances which supply much heat or do heavy work draw greater currents. A typical household may have 20 or 30 appliances, but fortunately only a few are used at any one time. The exact value of current drawn by an appliance or information from which this value can be determined is supplied on a name tag affixed to the appliance, or this information may be engraved on the appliance itself.

From the information in Table 9-1, it is possible to "design" the house wiring for a typical home. One possible arrangement is shown in Figure 9-7. Each line in this figure represents a two- or three-wire electrical line. A three-wire service line connects the distribution box to the main power line. The service line is rated for 100 amperes and has a 100-ampere fuse or circuit breaker in series with it. The service line also passes through the electric meter before entering the box so that the amount of energy used may be deter-

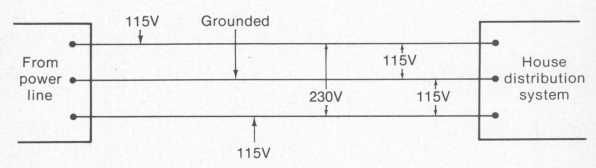

Fig. 9-6. Three-wire service line.

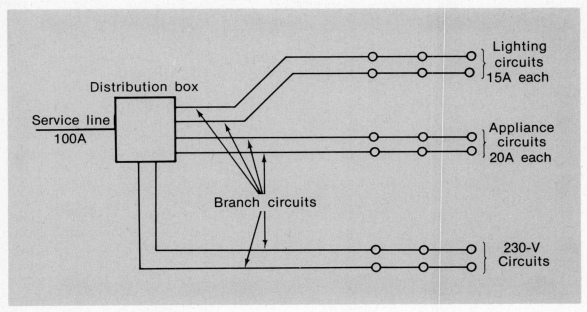

Fig. 9-7. Typical wiring arrangement.

mined. Several branch circuits emerge from the distribution box, and these are rated and fused according to their use. The *lighting*

Table 9-1. Typical Current Requirements

Appliances	Current Drawn (amperes)
100-watt bulb	0.9 amp
Phonograph	0.5
Television set	1.6
Refrigerator	2.0
Small fan	0.5
Blender	2.5
Juicer	2
Vacuum cleaner	6.0
Freezer	5.0
Garbage disposer	7.5
Dishwasher	12
Clothes dryer	20
Toaster	12
Iron	10
Space heater	14
Waffle iron	12

circuits are rated at 15 amperes each. These are wired throughout the house for lamps, small fans, electric razors and toothbrushes, radios and television sets. One branch line may service two or three rooms. A better arrangement is to have one branch for over-head lights and one or more for wall outlets in living room and bedrooms. Since heavier loads are required in the kitchen, the *appliance* circuits leading there are rated at 20 amperes each. The overhead lights in the kitchen should be on one of the 15-ampere circuits. The 230-volt branches are used for high-power equipment, and a separate branch should be used for each 230-volt appliance, such as the clothes dryer, air conditioner and range.

If too many appliances operate on a single circuit simultaneously, the total current drawn can exceed the safe rating of the wire. To prevent overheating and possible fires from excessive current, each branch has a fuse or circuit breaker which is designed to open the circuit when the rated current is exceeded. If an appliance has a short circuit, it will draw excessive current, since the short presents a lower resistance path across the line than the regular circuit. This will blow a fuse or open a circuit breaker. However, an open circuit breaker or blown fuse may also result when too many appliances are connected on one circuit, so that the total current drawn exceeds the rating of the circuit. Overloading is not usually dangerous, but it can be a nuisance.

9-2. Safety

WARNING: ELECTRICITY CAN BE LETHAL! This is something you must keep in mind whenever you do electrical work. If you pay attention to what you are doing, there is not the least danger, but if you allow yourself to be distracted or are careless, you may be in trouble. As long as you understand the danger, it is easy to avoid it.

One side of the house line is grounded, that is, firmly attached to the physical earth. The cold-water pipe in your home is also grounded, and if the hot-water pipe is connected to the cold, as through a common faucet, the hot-water pipe is also at ground potential. This is done for safety reasons, since if the electrical line were allowed to "float", there could be a very large voltage between the line and ground, even though the two wires in the line were only 115 volts apart. Large appliances should be physically grounded, especially if they are near water pipes. To do this, a wire is attached to a bare spot on the appliance, such as under the head of a screw, and the other end is attached to a water pipe by means of a grounding clamp. If you disconnect this ground connection to repair or move the appliance, make sure to connect it again before plugging in the appliance. Probably nothing will happen if you fail to do this, but there is always a remote possibility that the insulation on the line cord could be worn enough to permit the hot side of the line to contact the case of the appliance. If that happened and you touched the case and a water pipe, you would get a shock. When the case is grounded, this cannot

happen. A contact between the hot side of the line and the grounded case would blow a fuse, but there would be no danger of shock.

As mentioned in the preceding section, every electrical line in your home is protected by a fuse or circuit breaker to prevent too much current from flowing. Too much current can cause wires to get hot enough to start a fire. When a fuse blows or a circuit breaker opens, it is usually a sign of either an overload or a defective appliance. If the fuse blows as soon as an appliance or lamp is switched on, it is usually a sign of a short circuit in the device. You can replace the fuse (or reset the circuit breaker), but the circuit will be broken again if you try to turn on the defective appliance. If the circuit opens because of an overload, there will be a few seconds or even minutes delay between the time the last appliance was turned on and the circuit was broken. The solution is to move one or more appliances to another circuit.

If a circuit breaker is used to protect a circuit and it shuts off, it is simple to flick the switch back to reset it. If a fuse is used, however, when it blows it must be replaced. Do not try to bypass a fuse by placing metal foil or a penny under it. This is dangerous, since the line is then not protected against too much current.

When you are working on a circuit, you should shut off the electricity to that circuit. You can do this by unscrewing one of the fuses controlling that circuit, without affecting the operation of electrical appliances on other circuits. This is preferable to shutting off the main switch, but if you are not sure which fuses control the circuit you want to work on, play it safe by pulling the main switch.

To eliminate the necessity of shutting off all the electricity to make a repair, take the trouble to learn what fuses control which circuits. To do this, simply turn on lights and plug lamps in receptacles and then remove fuses (or open circuit breakers) one at a time. Each time you remove a fuse, some lights will go out, identifying the circuits controlled by that fuse. Record the information on a card or piece of paper, and put the record in the fuse box so it will be there when you need it.

9-3. How to Replace a Wall Switch

When you flip on a wall switch and nothing happens, the bulb may be burned out, the fuse may be burned out or the switch itself may be defective. Before rushing out to buy a new switch, make sure that the bulb and fuse are both all right. If your house has circuit breakers instead of fuses, check to see that the circuit breaker for the troublesome switch is in the *on* position. If everything else is working, you can suspect the switch.

The visible part of a switch is a wall plate with a rectangular hole through which a plastic lever protrudes. Figure 9-8 shows what is under the wall plate. The plate is held on by two screws which are screwed into two corresponding holes in the switch itself, as shown by the dotted lines. The switch is also held in the junction box by two screws. Two

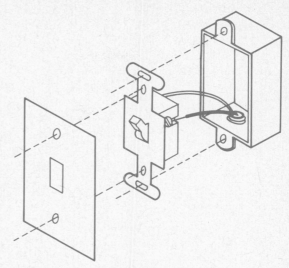

Fig. 9-8. Wall switch.

wires are connected to the switch terminals, which are screws with large heads. To get at

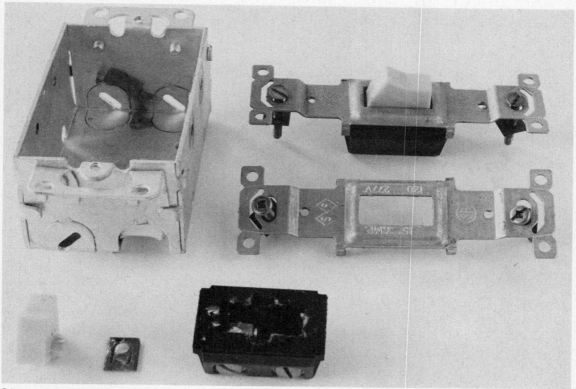

Disassembled wall switch.

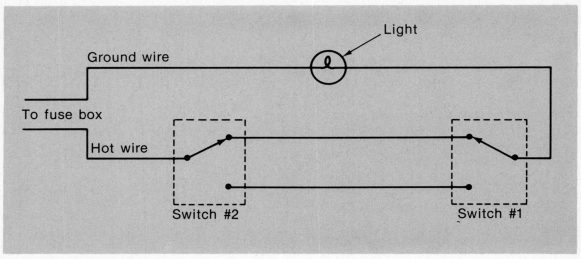

Fig. 9-9. Three-way switches.

the switch, first disconnect the electricity by pulling the proper fuse or shutting off the proper circuit breaker. If you are not sure which fuse controls the circuit, shut off the main switch. Now remove the screws holding the wall plate, and take off the wall plate. If the plate is stuck because of paint, pry it off with a knife or screwdriver. Remove the two screws holding the switch in the junction box and pull the switch out of the box. The wires attached to the switch are usually quite stiff, but don't be afraid to pull the switch out, since the wires will give. If either of these wires is loose, that could be the source of the trouble. Tighten the terminal screws, push the switch lever to the *on* position, and turn on the electricity again (put back the fuse or turn the circuit breaker on). If the light controlled by the switch goes on, the trouble was a loose connection. Shut off the electricity again, push the switch back into the junction box, and put all the screws and the wall plate back as they were. Turn the electricity on, and you are finished.

If there is no loose connection, the switch itself is probably faulty. When the switch is in the *on* position, it is supposed to make an electrical connection between the two wires attached to its terminals. Thus, you should be able to turn on the lights simply by bringing the two wires together. This is, in fact, how you check the switch. With the electricity

disconnected, remove one wire from the switch and hook it over the other wire at a bare spot. Better still, fasten both wires under a single screw so that they make a good electrical connection. Now turn on the electricity by putting back the fuse, and the lights should go on. This shows there is nothing wrong with the rest of the circuit, so the switch must be at fault.

To replace a switch, simply buy a new one and install it in the same manner. These switches are available with the switch lever in a variety of colors, so that you can pick one to match the decor in the room. Instead of the common snap-action switch, you may decide on one of the new special switches. Mercury switches look just like the common snap-action switches but are silent. In a bedroom or bathroom you may want a noiseless switch, and the mercury switch is the answer. Another type of switch has a push button instead of a lever. A dimmer switch has a knob which can be turned to make the lights dim or bright. The best part of working with any of these switches is that they all fit in the same junction box, and changing from a snap-action switch to any other type is simply a matter of removing a few screws and then putting them back.

Where two or more switches are close together, it is common practice to place them in one large junction box and cover them with a larger wall plate with the proper openings. Wall plates are usually made of thin metal, but you can also buy them made of wood or plastic and in a variety of shapes and designs.

In a large room or long hallway, it is usually desirable to be able to turn on the lights from two locations at opposite ends of the room. To do this, it is necessary to use special switches called *three-way* switches. These look like the simple *on-off* switch in Figure 9-8, except that they have three screw terminals, and three wires come out of the junction box. The electrical circuit is shown in Figure 9-9. The ground wire from the fuse box runs to the light controlled by the switches. A wire runs from the light to the first switch, and two wires run between the two switches. The second switch is connected to the hot side of the fuse box. When the switches are connected to the same wire, as shown in the figures, the circuit is closed and current flows, lighting the lamp. If either switch is thrown to the other wire, the circuit is interrupted and the light goes out. If one of the switches breaks, you must replace it with another three-way switch.

9-4. How to Replace a Receptacle

In your home you probably have wall receptacles in every room of the house for plugging in lamps and appliances. The common type of receptacle is shown in Figure 9-4. Receptacles rarely become defective, but when the internal springs or contacts wear, appliance cords may fall out, and you may want to replace the receptacle. Also, if you have small children in the home, you may want to install *safety receptacles*. These have slots that close when an appliance cord is removed, so that it is impossible for a child to stick a piece of metal into an empty receptacle. Changing a receptacle is as easy as changing a switch. First, shut off the electricity. Remove the one screw holding the wall plate in place. The receptacle is held in the junction box in

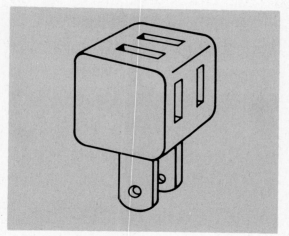
Fig. 9-10. Three-way plug.

exactly the same way as the switch. Remove the two screws holding it to the junction box, as shown in Figure 9-8 for the switch. Then remove the two wires from the terminals of the old receptacle and fasten them to the terminals of the new receptacle. Reassemble and turn on the electricity again.

There are times when you would like to plug three or more appliances into one receptacle and are faced with the problem of three cords to plug in but only two jacks. First of all, this is a bad practice and you shouldn't do it, but if you *must*, you can use a three-way plug, illustrated in Figure 9-10. This is plugged into a receptacle and in effect changes one jack to three. When you do this, make sure that the sum of all the current drawn by the various appliances does not exceed the rating of the circuit. Thus, in a 15-ampere circuit, for example, it is safe to have a phonograph, a television set and a lamp. (Current ratings are shown in Table 9-1.) However, if you had a space heater on the circuit, it might not be safe to add any other appliance.

9-5. Cords and Connectors

An extension cord enables you to bring electricity to a point where there is no

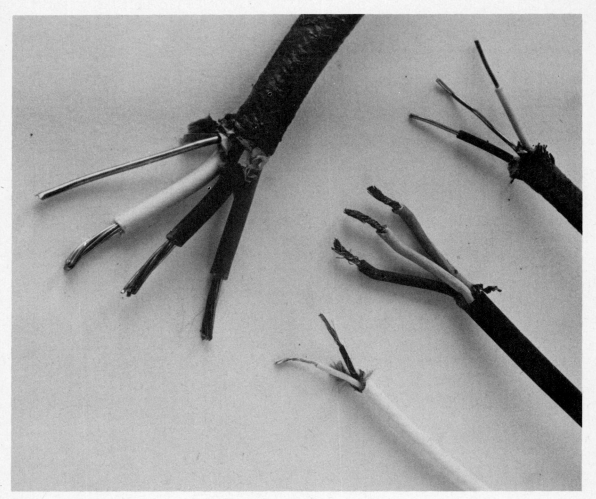

Types of electrical cord.

electrical outlet. It consists of a two-wire cord with a plug on one end and one or more jacks on the other. For home use, extension cords are available from 6 to 25 feet, and longer cords are available for industrial applications. Most extension cords will handle 10 amperes and can be used with a vacuum cleaner, for example. However, if you want to use a toaster or a waffle iron in your dining room and need an extension cord to reach an outlet, make sure the cord is heavy enough to take the current. To be safe, read the power on the appliance and divide by 100 to get a current rating with about a 10 per cent margin of safety. Thus, a 1500-watt toaster would be rated 15 amperes. The extension cord used

with it should be capable of handling this current. To satisfy most home applications, it is a good idea to have one 20-ampere extension cord and a few 10-ampere cords.

The cord on an appliance is called a *line cord*. Since line cords and extension cords must be flexible to go around objects or to permit movement (with vacuum cleaners and irons, for example), they are always made of stranded wire. If a single solid wire were used for each conductor, it would have to be large enough to carry the current required by the appliance. For most appliances, the wire size required could be achieved only in a stiff wire. Thinner wire is flexible but will not carry enough current without overheating. How-

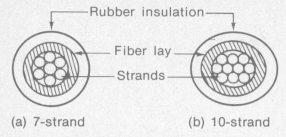

(a) 7-strand   (b) 10-strand

Fig. 9-11. Stranded conductor with wrapping.

ever, if several thin wires (or strands) are grouped together in a single conductor, they share the current equally and thus can carry heavier currents without overheating. All line cords use stranded conductors. Cross sections of individual conductors are shown in Figure 9-11. Each conductor consists of a bundle of strands of thin wire. This bundle is tightly enclosed with a wrapping of fiber, called a *lay*, and then covered with rubber insulation. There are several different types of line cords, but all those used with home appliances have the conductors wrapped in fiber and rubber (Figure 9-11). The more popular line cords have conductors with seven or ten strands, but for heavy-duty installations, wires with as many as 65 strands in each conductor are used.

When you strip insulation from a conductor in a line cord, it is important that you do not cut into any of the strands. If you break a few strands, the appliance will operate properly, but each of the remaining strands will carry more current than it should. For example, suppose that a toaster which draws 10 amperes has a line cord with ten-strand conductors, as shown in Figure 9-11. Each strand then carries only 1 ampere, and these strands can be relatively thin wires. However, if six strands break because of too much flexing or poor installation, the remaining four will have to carry the 10-ampere load, and each will carry 2.5 amperes. This will cause the line cord to get hot near the break. You

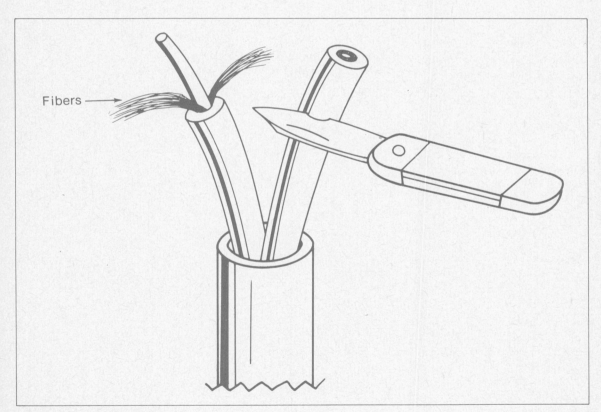

Fig. 9-12. Stripping insulation.

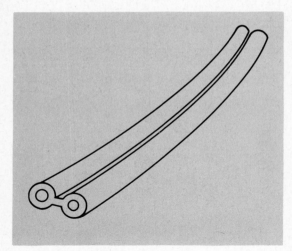

Fig. 9-13. Zipcord.

can use a jackknife to strip insulation, but you should not use too much force. Cut into the insulation *lightly* by rotating the knife around the wire about 1 inch from the end, as shown in Figure 9-12. When the insulation is cut all the way around, the severed portion can be pulled off like a sleeve. The fiber lay between the strands and the rubber insulation protects the strands from the knife, and there should be little risk of cutting the wire strands if the

job is done carefully. After pulling off the sleeve, the fiber lay can be unwrapped, as shown on the conductor at the left in Figure 9-12, and can be cut off with scissors or a knife.

For most low-power appliances, such as clocks, juicers and lamps, which draw fewer than 2 or 3 amperes, the most common type of line cord is the popular *zipcord* (Figure 9-13). This consists of two conductors, like those in Figure 9-11, joined together by a thin rubber bond. It is called "zipcord", because the two conductors are easily separated by tearing the thin rubber membrane joining them.

For heavier work, such as mixers and vacuum cleaners, *jacketed cable* is used. The wrapped conductors are separated by additional fibers which increase the insulation between them, both electrical and thermal. The two conductors and extra fibers are encased in a rubber or plastic jacket. This type is called SV cord, and its construction is shown in Figure 9-14. In general, jacketed cable will take more abuse than zipcord.

For appliances which draw more than 5 amperes, special *heater cord* is preferred. This is used on toasters, waffle irons, irons

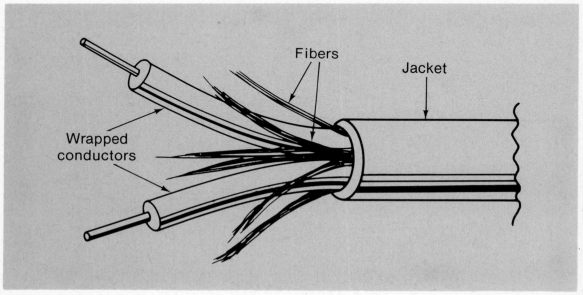

Fibers

Jacket

Wrapped
conductors

Fig. 9-14. SV Cord.

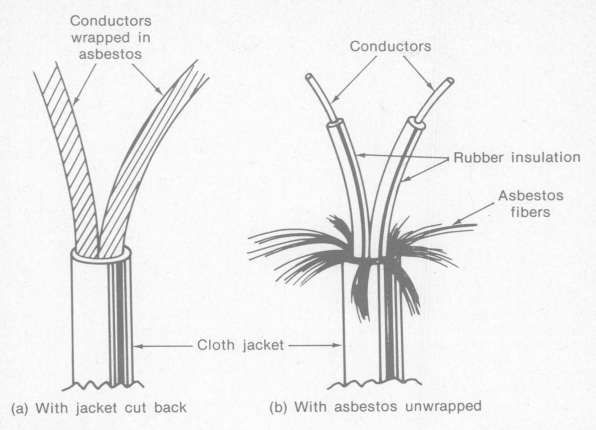

Fig. 9-15. Heater cord.

and other appliances that provide heat rather than motion. In heater cord, each wrapped conductor shown in Figure 9-11 is also wrapped with asbestos fibers. Then the two conductors are brought together and a layer of asbestos is wrapped around both. Finally, the package is encased in a braided jacket of cotton or nylon. Heater cord is illustrated in Figure 9-15.

The current-carrying capacity of the line cord depends on the wire diameter and not on the insulation. Thus, a zipcord line with #10 wire can carry 25 amperes, whereas an asbestos heater cord with #18 may be limited to 5 or 6 amperes. Nevertheless, in general, heater cords are used for appliances that draw more current; jacketed cable is used where the cord itself is subject to abuse; and zipcord is by far the most common because of its simplicity and is used wherever there are no special demands on the line cord.

When a cord is shortened or replaced, a plug has to be attached to it. It is important to connect a cord to a plug so that the connection will not be under strain when the cord is pulled. When attaching a cord to a plug, you can remove strain from the connections by tying a knot in the line cord after passing it through the connector. The typical "Underwriters' knot" is shown in Figure 9-16. First, slip the plug over the line cord, as in Figure 9-16(a). The first loop of the knot is shown in Figure 9-16(b), with the rest of the knot indicated by a dotted line. The knot is slid down to the end of the insulation. Any kind of knot will do as long as it prevents the cord from being pulled out of the plug. The two wires are now stripped, passed around the blades of the plug, and the stripped portion tightened under the mounting screws as shown in Figure 9-16(c). The wire should not be crossed over itself under a screw, as tightening may cause it to break.

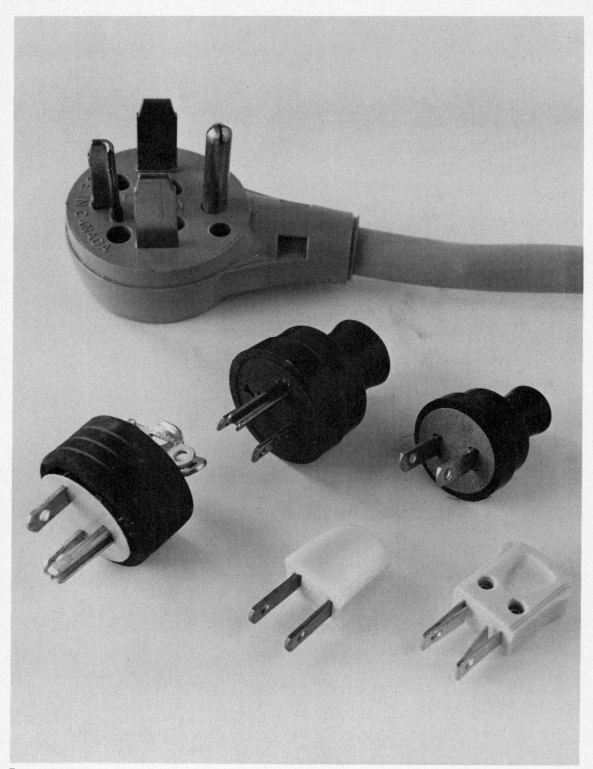

Types of plugs.

(c) Connected

(a) Plug slipped over cord

(b) Knot

Fig. 9-16. Strain-relieving knot.

If the appliance draws fewer than 2 amperes and has a zipcord line cord, you can use a gripper plug. Here there is no strain-relieving knot, no stripping of wire and no contact screws. Although the connection can be damaged by jerking the line cord, with reasonable care it can give adequate service indefinitely. There are many varieties of gripper plugs on the market, and all come with simple instructions for installing.

WARNING: *Do not use on anything but zipcord* and in low-current applications.

Extension cords and line cords should last indefinitely if they are not abused. You should never pull a plug out of an outlet by yanking on the cord. There may be no apparent damage, but continued yanking can break some of the strands of wire. Never run extension cords where they can be stepped on, such as under a rug, or squashed, such as under a door. The unusual pressure can damage the insulation, causing a hazardous situation. Never run cords next to metal surfaces, especially near hot radiators. Heat can dry out the insulation, causing it to crack, and the cord may then short-circuit to the metal surface. Never use tacks or staples to hold cords along moldings or door frames, since insulation can be damaged. However, it is all right to hang a cord on hooks along a molding. A better way is to buy a special outlet strip which attaches to a molding and provides receptacles at any point on the molding.

9-6. Doorbells

The basic circuits for a doorbell are shown in Figure 9-17. A bell transformer is connected permanently to the 115-volt house line. This transforms the voltage to a safe low value, usually about 12 volts for a bell or buzzer and up to 24 volts for a set of chimes. The push buttons, then, are located in low-voltage lines, reducing the danger of electric shock. Because these wires have a low-voltage difference, they can be run in walls and under floors without the precautions required for the 115-volt line.

In Figure 9-17(a), a circuit for a single push

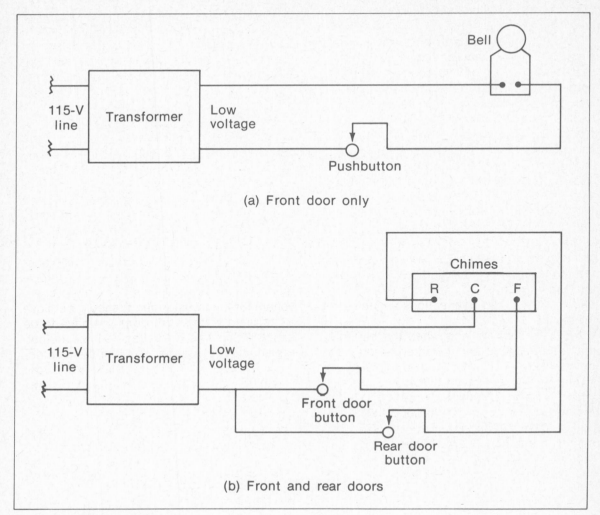

Fig. 9-17. Doorbell circuits.

button is shown. When the button is pushed, the circuit is closed, and the bell rings. In Figure 9-17(b), a circuit using chimes and two push buttons is shown. There are two separate circuits, each controlled by a different push button. Two different chimes are used to differentiate between front and back doors. The letters R, C and F stand for "rear", "common" and "front", respectively.

If you have bells or buzzers in your home and wish to install chimes instead, you may have to change the transformer. The voltage output of the transformer is marked on the nameplate, but you must find the transformer. It is usually near the fuse box. When you buy a

set of chimes that suits you, notice what voltage is required, and if your present transformer is inadequate, you will have to buy a new transformer to go with the chime set. If the front and rear bells are close together, it is easy to remove them and transfer the wires to a chime set. You will have to trace the wires back to the transformer to find which are the common ones. In Figure 9-18, the common wire at each bell is labeled C, and the other wires are labeled F and R (for front and rear). Simply attach one of the C wires to the center terminal of the chime set. You can cut off the other common wire. Connect the F and R wires to the indicated terminals on the chime set (these are usually labeled). The job is done.

If the front bell and rear buzzer are widely separated, you will have to run a wire from one push button to the chime set. For example, you place the chime set at the front doorbell. Now you must run a wire from the rear button to the chime. If you wish, you can pull the old rear buzzer wire out of the wall and use it, or you can leave it, but disconnect it from the push button. To run a wire up to the chime set, tie a long piece of string to a wire already there. Then go into the cellar and pull that wire out of the wall so that the string is inside the wall instead. Make sure that an end of the string still protrudes from the wall near the chime. Now attach a second wire to the end of the string in the cellar, and pull both wires back up into the wall by pulling the upper end of the string. Make connections as indicated in Figure 9-17(b).

If a bell does not ring when the button is pushed (assuming that it worked before), the trouble may be in the fuse box, the transformer, the wires, the push button or the bell itself. The most common source of trouble is the push button. Remove the cover from the button either by taking out two screws or by prying with a small screwdriver if no screws are visible. You will see two wires which should be firmly attached to terminals on the

push button. Remove these two wires and touch them together. If the bell rings, the trouble is definitely the push button. Cleaning the contacts with sandpaper is usually all that is required. However, a new push button is inexpensive and is easily installed in place of a defective one.

If touching the wires together does not cause the bell to ring, check the *output* of the bell transformer. WARNING: Be careful not to touch the input or primary side of the transformer, since that side has 115 volts across it. The input side has two heavy wires connected to it, whereas the output side has two thin wires. Touch a screwdriver blade across the two transformer output terminals momentarily. There should be a spark if the transformer is in good condition. Alternatively, if you have a voltmeter, you can measure the output voltage of the transformer. It should be close to its rated voltage but does not have to be exact. If there is no voltage at the output, replace the transformer. Shut off the electricity when you do this, and connect the four wires on the new transformer to the same points that the four old wires were connected. For best results, solder the connections, and put insulating tape over each soldered joint. You can also use solderless connectors, which look like black thimbles. These are threaded onto a pair of wires twisted together

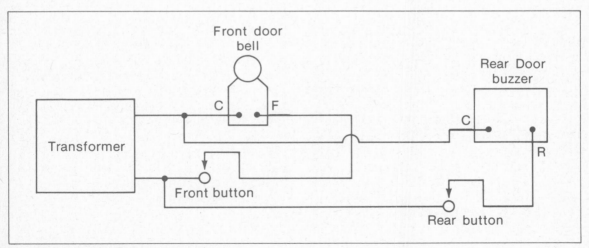

Fig. 9-18. Separate front and rear bells.

and serve to hold the wires firmly and to insulate them at the same time.

If the transformer and push button are all right, check the wires. If insulation wears on a pair of wires, they may rub together and cause a short circuit. If you find bare spots on wires, cover them with insulating tape.

Finally, if all else seems to be working, the trouble may be the bell itself. If you have a voltmeter, check the voltage at the bell with someone holding in the push button. If no one else is around, remove the wires from the button and twist them together when you make this voltage test. If you do not have a voltmeter, remove the two wires from the bell and touch them together momentarily while the push button is held in or the wires are twisted together. There should be a spark indicating voltage at the bell terminals. If there is voltage and the bell does not work, try cleaning the contacts with sandpaper. If this doesn't cure the trouble, the coils may be burned out, and the easiest solution is to replace the bell.

Since bell systems are usually on low-voltage circuits, it is not necessary to take precautions against electric shock, except when working at the bell transformer. Nevertheless, it is dangerous to be too complacent, and you should approach all wiring cautiously, and ask yourself what voltage is on the line you will be touching.

Some bell systems operate off a battery instead of a transformer and are thus completely separate from the house electric circuit. Such a system cannot have a burned out transformer, but it can have a dead battery. You can check a battery by placing a bulb of the proper voltage rating across its terminals. If the bulb lights, the battery is working. Note that an ordinary 115-volt bulb will not light when placed across a 6-volt battery, so it is necessary to use the proper bulb.